MIND SHIFT. PROFIT LIFT.

Rewiring Your Entrepreneurial Brain for Greater Profitability, Growth, & Staying Power

PETER RICCIARDI

Ten9Eight7 LLC

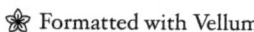 Formatted with Vellum

CONTENTS

SECTION 4
Run Your Business without Losing Control.

SECTION 5
Determine How Customers Best Experience You.

FINAL OBSERVATIONS AND TAKEAWAYS

"The most dangerous phrase in the language is 'We've always done it this way.'"
—*Grace Hopper*

MEET PETER RICCIARDI

Business Advisor. Entrepreneur. Speaker.

Most careers follow a timeline.

Peter Ricciardi's didn't.

He graduated cum laude with a Wharton courseload from the University of Pennsylvania at age nineteen.

Then he returned to his former high school and taught economic history to seniors before turning twenty.

That is not normal. It is also not accidental.

By twenty-five, Peter became the youngest Burger King franchisee in company history.

Before thirty, he was invited into the prestigious New England Regional Business Council.

Then he did what he has always done best. He went where the profit was leaking. And fixed it.

In his thirties, Peter launched his consulting career by transforming food and beverage operations at what still today is the most successful day-and-night ski area in the country. The results were so clear, he was invited twice to speak at the National Ski Convention, addressing dozens of operators from well-known resorts on improving food and beverage profitability.

The ski area quickly saw more than numbers. They saw judgment. So they expanded his role into marketing and branding strategy.

Next came sports.

Peter spearheaded the highly successful launch and operation of pro hockey in a city where pro sports franchises had previously gone to die. After helping to bring on another AHL team, he was hand-selected to serve as Team President of one of only 8 NBA-owned G League teams at the time.

But here is the part that matters most.

He came back to the work that actually moves businesses forward: Helping small and mid-sized companies operate more profitably, more intentionally, and more sustainably.

No hype. Just discipline.

No gimmicks. Just counterintuitive thinking.

Over time, his impact expanded well beyond hospitality and professional sports. He has advised leaders across technology, software, ecosolutions, beverage, franchise, digital marketing, and recreational vehicles.

He has been invited to lecture on marketing and profitability at colleges and universities.

Today, Peter consults selectively.

He works with leaders who are willing to challenge assumptions, confront reality, and rethink how they run their businesses.

Because the old way is not just outdated. It is expensive.

This book is a broader platform to share the lessons, missteps, and insights he earned along the way.

Peter sincerely hopes you are one of those business leaders willing to rethink what's possible. Because lifting profit comes from thinking differently, not doing more.

THANK YOU...

To Blake, without your encouragement and perspective, I would never have taken this leap.

To Vicki, for unselfishly sharing both your time and your prowess as a respected author.

To Ben and Summer, for always being there in countless ways.

To George, for seamlessly joining our journey.

And to my dearest Kathleen, for your unwavering support, patience, and belief, as the all-in spouse of a lifelong entrepreneur.

A NOTE FROM THE AUTHOR

I didn't write *Mind Shift. Profit Lift.* to impress you.

Not with complicated theories. Not with business jargon. Not with academic frameworks.

And I'm not claiming to have all the answers.

What I do have, earned over years working alongside entrepreneurs and business leaders, is a deep respect for the questions most people never think to ask...or choose to ignore.

Usually because the answers feel wrong at first. Because they run against what we've been taught. What feels safe. What "everyone else" is doing.

But those are the questions that matter most.

This book is not for you if you want hacks, shortcuts, or a list of tactics you can try for a week and forget. It will be of little value if what you really want is validation instead of responsibility.

Because this book is built around counterintuitive insights and real-world stories that challenge conventional thinking about business, profitability, and success.

They are designed to make you pause. To rethink what you have assumed. To see your opportunities and obstacles through a sharper lens.

Many of you will want to push back. To challenge what feels like a new way of approaching business principles you've long held dear. That is to be expected. But it is also the first step in the process I hope you engage in after reading this book.

I am certain that whether you have owned a family business for decades, took the entrepreneurial leap a few years ago, or are still deciding if you are ready, these ideas will meet you where you are.

My goal is simple.

I want this to feel less like a lecture and more like a conversation over coffee with someone who has been in the trenches. Approachable. Worth your time. Useful from page one.

So let's start here.

How do I define an entrepreneur?

Entrepreneur (n.): Someone who takes responsibility for initiating and/or improving a product, service, system, business, experience, or outcome.

Entrepreneurship is not a title. It is not a business card. It is not even ownership.

It is a mindset.

If you make decisions that affect customers, revenue, people, or performance, you are already practicing entrepreneurship.

If you solve problems, challenge assumptions, take initiative, and look for better ways to create value, you will recognize yourself in the pages ahead.

Parts of this book speak directly to business owners. But I did not write it only for them.

If you take ownership of your impact, feel accountable for outcomes (not just tasks), and care about doing things better tomorrow than you did today, this book was written for you, too.

Now let's get started, OK?

SECTION 1

Think Like a Highly Profitable Entrepreneur.

#1 GET UNSTUCK.

"Profit is the applause you get for taking care of your customers and creating value." —*Ken Blanchard*

This book isn't about starting a business.

It's about making the one you already have work the way it should.

It's written for owners and business leaders who are doing most things "right," working hard, staying busy, staying committed, and yet still feeling like something isn't adding up.

Revenue may be growing. Effort is undeniable. Yet profit, clarity, or control stubbornly lag behind.

If you believe hard work alone guarantees success, this book will challenge you.

If you suspect that pricing, positioning, discipline, and decision-making, not effort, are determining your results, then this book was written for you.

But before you revisit pricing, costs, margins, or growth, you must fix the way you think about business.

That is a great deal more challenging than changing tactics. It requires opening your mind and embracing ideas that may feel uncomfortable, even counterintuitive.

Because we entrepreneurs are a fascinating group. Driven. Independent. Confident. Convinced we can figure out almost anything. Most of us don't want a boss. And many of us believe, sometimes to a fault, that we already know exactly how to make our businesses highly profitable.

If that sounds like you, good. You're in the right place.

As powerful as that confidence can be, it often comes with blind spots big enough to cap your growth or choke your bottom line. And those blind spots can show up at any point in your journey.

So why are these blind spots so common?

Simple. Too many of us have bought into long-accepted business "truisms," many of which aren't so true. Many of which are actually moving you further away from your goals.

The mind shift I'm encouraging starts with what you believe your business is actually about. So let's get this out of the way early.

Rule #1: Your business is not about you. Not even a little.

It's not about your opinions, your assumptions, your tastes, your preferences, your family, your partners, or your investors.

It's about them.

The people who choose to buy from you. Or choose not to.

It's about their needs. Their expectations. Their frustrations. Their wants. And their version of "better." Not yours.

If you do not consistently meet or exceed those expectations, your chances of long-term success are essentially zero.

And yet every day, business owners who swear they "get" the importance of the customer make decisions that ignore the customer entirely.

Still not buying it?

Then how do we explain blind spots like these:

• Customer service treated as a nice-to-have instead of the core differentiator

- Energy poured into chasing new customers while loyal customers get ignored
- Pricing determined by what something costs instead of the value the customer perceives
- Strategies built around an accountant's logic instead of the market's reality
- Few, if any, real ways for customers to provide honest feedback
- Intentionally deceiving product descriptions and sneaky auto-renewals
- Hidden fees designed to trick the consumer or client

And the most dangerous blind spot of all?

Thinking the primary purpose of your business is to make a profit.

It's not. That's the result.

The purpose is to meet and exceed the expectations of the people who give you the privilege of serving them.

Done well, profit follows. Done exceptionally well, profit lifts off.

Done poorly, there is always room on the scrap heap for one more failed business. And it's a pretty big heap, already, without your business joining it.

If any of this is starting to hit home, good.

If you've always believed this all-important mindset was second nature to you, great. Your feedback is welcomed.

You'll discover quickly that this book is not an exercise in business theory. Rather, it is a collection of real strategies, real insights, real stories, and real evidence drawn from decades of working in and with businesses of every size.

If you're ready to rethink what you sell, why you sell it, how you price it, how you deliver it, and even the very business you think you're in, then turn the page.

All you've got to lose is yesterday's baggage. And in today's world, your baggage certainly doesn't fly free anymore.

S2L (Shift to Lift): You cannot lift results with a closed mind. If your assumptions stay the same, your outcomes will, too. This book will only be impactful after you commit to thinking differently.

#2 ACKNOWLEDGE WHO COMES NEXT.

"If you want loyal customers, start by creating loyal employees." —*Mac Anderson*

If you still believe your business exists to serve you, this chapter will challenge you. It may even frustrate you.

Not only do you not come first, neither do your partners or investors. After your customers come your employees.

I am not spouting philosophy. I am simply sharing operational reality. Customers are the reason your business exists.

And your employees are the reason your customers stay.

When employees are trained, motivated, empowered, and supported, customer experience lifts naturally. When they are ignored, undervalued, or merely tolerated, it drags or collapses just as predictably.

This is often why businesses with similar products, prices, and markets perform so differently. You might think the difference is strategy. It's not.

It's how seriously leadership treats the people who show up every day to represent the business when no one, including you, is watching.

So why do so many business owners treat employees like a necessary evil?

Why would any entrepreneur believe customers will be delighted if the staff is simply surviving, not thriving?

It's ironic, isn't it? As entrepreneurs, we proudly call these "our businesses," yet success has everything to do with others.

Those we serve. Those we hire. Those we keep. Those we coach.

And especially those who represent us when we're not in the room.

Your employees are not an expense to manage. They are the engine that either amplifies or suffocates the customer experience you claim to care about.

When you invest in your team, they invest in your customers. When you ignore them, they ignore your customers.

It's that simple. And that costly.

S2L: Customer loyalty is a direct byproduct of employee loyalty. If your people are disengaged, unsupported, or merely surviving, your customers will feel it. And your margins will pay for it. Treat employees like an expense, and watch your customers treat you like a commodity.

#3 ACT WITH PURPOSE.

"Excellence is never an accident; it's the result of high intention, sincere effort, and intelligent execution." — *Aristotle*

The more time I spend working with entrepreneurs, the more I realize how much in their businesses simply happens. Not by intention, not by design...it just happens.

Running a business is hard. What surprises me most is how many big and not-so-big decisions get made "just because."

Just because no one expected that particular situation to show up.

Just because no one anticipated two key employees being out at the same time.

Just because no one realized a weather spike could double product demand overnight.

Just because no one created a protocol for answering the phone or handling a sudden supply shortage until the moment it happened.

As you work your way through this guide, *my hope is that it pushes you to eliminate as many accidental decisions as possible.* That doesn't mean building a 500-page manual or creating a company rulebook longer than 25 CVS receipts. It does mean having a clear company mantra, open internal communication, and a commitment to ongoing training. And it absolutely means committing to consistent execution.

One thing never changes. Consistently delighting customers requires a unified team effort, empowered employees, individual accountability at every level, and a relentless desire to improve. Customers might find you by accident, but returning and recommending you happens for one reason only...because of what you do and what you don't.

S2L: Profit doesn't grow by accident. Purpose drives it every time.

#4 LOVE WHAT YOU DO.

"I'd rather fail believing in something than succeed at something I didn't believe in." —*Todd Graves*

Merriam-Webster defines passion as "a powerful or compelling enthusiasm or interest in something." I couldn't agree more. Passion fuels staying power. It fuels perseverance. It fuels success. Yet I continue to meet entrepreneurs who have little respect for the very products they sell or the services they offer. It baffles me every time.

I once worked with an avowed vegetarian who was eager to open and operate a steakhouse in a market he felt "needed one." That's an absolutely true story. Who could possibly make that up?

I've watched friends who love banking and retail clothing settle for buying a restaurant franchise. I've had conversations with corporate lifers who suddenly wanted to open any type of business at all, as long as it might make them money, regardless of whether it aligned with their interests, strengths, or values.

Here's my advice. And it never wavers. Owning a business is incredibly demanding. Delighting customers today can be even more challenging than finding and retaining employees. Roadblocks, detours, and setbacks will show up regularly. Passionate entrepreneurs make it through. Entrepreneurs who chase only the money almost never do.

Follow only the cash, and your passion won't follow. When passion disappears, so does resilience. And when resilience disappears, your bottom line is limited at best and nonexistent at worst.

S2L: Being a successful entrepreneur is exceptionally demanding. Without real passion for the business, you are way more likely to give up long before you ever get to experience what could have been possible.

#5 TAP EVERY RESOURCE.

"When you know better, you do better." —*Maya Angelou*

Entrepreneurship can feel overwhelming long before you collect your first dollar. And even after a solid revenue year, it helps to remember this truth. You are far from the only business with limited cash. You are not the only one struggling to find skilled employees. And you are certainly not the only entrepreneur racing to leverage AI as a competitive advantage.

But here's what sets you apart. You have the power to learn. You have access to more experience, more expertise, and more wisdom than any business owner in history. Podcasts. YouTube. TED Talks. Affordable AI. Paid consultants. Business books like this. The list is endless.

Commit to learning. Commit to curiosity. Commit to leaning on others.

Most of all, commit to asking for help when you need it. Working with the equivalent of sound-deadening earmuffs on is dangerous. You won't just miss good advice. You won't hear the eighteen-wheeler barreling toward your company until it's too late.

S2L: If better profit is your goal, then gaining knowledge and motivation in every way possible should be non-negotiable.

#6 LEARN FROM THE MISSTEPS OF OTHERS.

"Learn from the mistakes of others. You can't live long enough to make them all yourself." —*Eleanor Roosevelt*

We all agree there's no reason to repeat the mistakes others have made. At least we should. Chances are you know several successful entrepreneurs, even if only as a customer or casual acquaintance. Most will gladly find an hour over coffee to act as a sounding board.

You may also know someone respected for helping others launch or grow small businesses. I've spent much of my professional life doing exactly that. Their experience can be invaluable if you're willing to listen. (And yes, I still make myself available when the fit makes sense.)

I once had a neighbor who was thriving in the financial world. He knew my extensive franchise background well. Thinking franchising offered an even more lucrative future, he asked me to evaluate two existing Popeyes locations for sale within an hour of his home. He was ready to pay me thousands to review the books and assess the sites.

My consulting gig lasted minutes, not weeks, because I knew the right question to ask.

"Are there any existing Popeyes franchisees near these restaurants?" I asked.

"Yes," he said. "Two."

My advice was immediate. "Walk away and keep your day job."

He looked disappointed. He really wanted to be a fried chicken mogul. But he listened.

Here's what I knew. No local operator passes up a chance to expand into a turnkey franchise opportunity unless they doubt the viability of that location. And sure enough, a short time later both those restaurants were boarded up. He later brought me an unexpected thank-you gift for saving him from a disastrous investment.

If you can learn from others, never hesitate. Just make sure the people you're learning from are the real deal.

S2L: Knowing you don't have all the answers isn't weakness. It's smart business. Be sure to keep this mindset on your radar at every stage of your entrepreneurial journey.

#7 LOOK CAREFULLY BEFORE LEAPING INTO A FRANCHISE.

"Facts do not cease to exist because they are ignored." — *Aldous Huxley*

It's hard not to have gathered substantial wisdom about franchising when you have my résumé. I have been a franchisee twice and a consultant to franchisors twice. I have also advised numerous franchisees and plenty of people considering becoming one.

This book is built on a simple, proven reality: a lot of people want to be entrepreneurs. Franchising often feels like the safest road to ownership because the brand exists, the playbook exists, and the systems exist.

Sometimes that's true.

But there are also risks you need to see clearly before you sign anything. Trust me, the reminders I am about to share are pure gold.

First, *one fact that surprises many: franchises do fail.* A recent Michigan Ross study found that the one-year survival rate for new franchised single-establishment businesses is only about 6.3 percentage points higher than for independent businesses. That's encouraging, but it's not a guarantee, and it's certainly not

indicative of a free pass to success. Remember when there was a
Cold Stone Creamery and a Quiznos on every corner? The key
word is 'remember.'

Ten things to be wary of before you buy:

1. *A brand can be strong somewhere else and weak where you
   live.* If the franchise is well-known in a market other
   than yours, you may be buying recognition you can't
   actually monetize.
2. *Your success can be limited by decisions you don't control.* If
   the franchisor's marketing is underfunded,
   inconsistent, or out of touch locally, you pay the price.
3. *Innovation can stop at the top.* When the franchisor
   stops innovating, the franchisee is forced to defend
   yesterday's model with today's costs.
4. *Brand trust can erode fast.* A scandal, quality slip, supply
   issue, or a poorly conceived or panicked corporate
   decision can hit every operator in the system, whether
   you caused it or not.
5. *Territories can be oversold.* If your territory is diluted by
   additional locations, your "potential" was never really
   yours in the first place.
6. *Standards can be lowered.* When a franchisor relaxes
   standards to grow unit count, every operator is
   dragged toward mediocrity.
7. *Franchise brokers are not your fiduciary.* Many prospective
   franchisees overestimate a broker's role. In most
   cases, a broker's primary incentive is a completed sale,
   often with higher commissions paid on certain
   brands. Your long-term success is often not even on
   their radar.
8. *Franchising does not reward creativity.* It rewards
   unanimity. Think you can "tweak" the formula or

improve the model? Think again. I experienced this firsthand. With a Burger King sitting in the blueberry capital of North America, after pushing hard, I was allowed to test blueberry pancakes. They were so successful I was forced to stop selling them. Why? Because customers began asking for them at other Burger King locations where they weren't available. Franchising rewards consistency for obvious reasons, but that consistency can also handcuff the best operators.

9. *Some franchisors are more focused on selling franchises than delighting customers.* When its core business becomes unit sales instead of customer obsession, both the franchisor and franchisee eventually pay for it. I have seen that happen up close and personal on multiple occasions.

10. *Franchisors get paid off top-line sales, not your bottom line.* Royalty structures typically tie to gross sales. That explains why they may pressure their franchisees to chase volume, sacrifice margins, discount too often, or run promotions that train customers to wait for deals. Great for top-line. Many times, brutal for your profit.

A few additional realities you should never forget:

• Be wary of absentee ownership systems. These arrangements can lead to a lack of oversight, resulting in operational issues that might go unnoticed until it's too late. If you're considering investing in a franchise, ensure you have a solid understanding of the business model and are prepared to be actively involved in its management. There is a reason the best brands are picky about operators. A poorly run franchise wearing your brand hurts your success, too.

• Never buy without talking to multiple existing franchisees in markets similar to yours. Disclosure rules often limit what can be promised, so you must do your own due diligence through operator conversations and real-world comparisons.

• Almost no franchisor guarantees your debt. They don't co-sign your loan, and they don't bail you out if your operation fails.

S2L: Don't assume anything when considering the franchise route. Do your due diligence, then do more. The right franchise can be a profit machine. Hooking up with the wrong franchisor can become an absolute nightmare.

#8 RESET YOUR MINDSET.

"What we fear doing most is usually what we most need to do." —*Tim Ferriss*

That quote sums up the mind shift I hope you're already feeling.

You and your business will benefit greatly from shifting the way you have previously looked at business.

That starts with meeting your new boss.

Your customer... your client... your subscriber... your follower.

Every action your company takes from this point forward must reflect that understanding. Their needs, their feelings, and their reactions now must sit at the center of your decision-making. You won't raise or lower a price, add or drop an item, or adjust a package without thinking through how it impacts their experience. And you will never forget that your employees must share this commitment if you expect to successfully and consistently deliver on your promise.

This is where real transformation begins.

New tools and tactics obviously matter. But a renewed mindset is what will unlock your superpower.

Thanks for your patience. Now let's get after it and focus on achieving real tangible results.

S2L: A new mindset isn't a small step. But it's the critical first step on the way to improved clarity, greater purpose, and an improved bottom line. Congrats!

SECTION 2

Define Value and Differentiate.

#9 RESEARCH, THEN INVEST.
NOT IN REVERSE ORDER.

"The essence of strategy is choosing what not to do." —
Michael E. Porter

Trust me, I am the last person who wants to squash the entrepreneurial spirit.

But this reality must be shared. Far too often, businesspeople get struck with what feels like a unique, game-changing idea for a new company or product. And sometimes it actually is. The problem is simple. *A niche and a hole look almost identical until you throw money at one.*

I have had a double-digit number of would-be entrepreneurs confidentially pitch their "can't miss" idea, fully convinced no one has ever thought of it. Honestly, I struggle to understand how they arrive at that conclusion unless their laptop somehow cannot access Google or ChatGPT.

You are not the first person to dream of a national hot dog franchise. You are not the first to believe a town of 3,500 can support its own hardware store. You are not the first to think a pizza place should add sushi. And you are certainly not the first to believe a warm-weather town desperately needs an expensive indoor tennis center.

More often than not, proper research reveals that seasoned fast-food operators, industry veterans, and savvy developers have already explored or avoided the very idea you see as original.

When someone comes to me bright-eyed and energized, I love it. That enthusiasm is contagious. But once they hire me, I have a fiduciary responsibility to ground their vision in facts. Unfortunately, too many entrepreneurs only learn those facts after burning through their savings or, worse, someone else's.

One story says it all.

A software client proudly showed me the "new" platform they were developing, convinced they had discovered white space in the market. They had not. And I discovered that fact for them just weeks into my consulting gig. What they were painstakingly building already existed in a far superior form and had for nearly two years. Heck, it was actually being used in a big way already.

What made it worse is that they stayed the course. They continued development. Really? Yep! They drained every investor dollar.

Who lost? Everyone. Especially the employees whose final paychecks never arrived.

Entrepreneurs are a different breed. But even the boldest among us must acknowledge reality. Plenty of people have lost their shirts chasing what they believed was a niche when it was actually a hole.

Real niches still exist. Truly innovative ideas still launch every year. But it is your responsibility to make sure your vision is not just a hole waiting to swallow your investment. Or your grandmother's savings.

S2L: There is no excuse for skipping your homework. Wasting your cash or your investor's when you could have known better is simply unacceptable.

#10 KNOW EXACTLY WHAT BUSINESS YOU'RE IN.

"People don't want a quarter-inch drill. They want a quarter-inch hole." —Theodore Levitt

Phil Knight turned Nike into an absolute profit machine not because he obsessed over athletic shoes, but because he understood something most entrepreneurs never fully grasp:

Your customers are not buying what you sell. *They are buying what it does for them.* And how it makes them feel.

Need proof? Look at a few prominent examples.

Buc-ee's knows it is far more than gas pumps and brisket sandwiches. It is a one-of-a-kind highway oasis. Its true product is relief. Clean bathrooms. A place that feels safe, bright, fun, and unmatched.

Bugatti understands a Kia will get you to the same destination in virtually the same amount of time. That is precisely why Bugatti is not really selling cars at all. They are selling identity, status, and membership in an elite club.

Walt Disney World has not been selling rides, stuffed animals, and Dole Whip for decades. They sell magic. Escape. Wonder. The chance to be a kid again. And again.

Apple has never forgotten its real responsibility. To get you to tomorrow before everyone else does. The product they have always delivered: the future.

Whole Foods was not built for people with appetites. It was built for people with intentions. People who care deeply about their bodies and their minds.

MetLife has never really sold life insurance. They sell peace of mind.

These companies know exactly what business they are in. Most have known it since day one. Do you?

Here is the real question you must answer. What is your customer actually achieving when they choose you?

Are they buying convenience?

Less stress?

A smile from their child?

Approval from their boss?

Comfort?

Confidence?

Time?

Relief?

The chance to impress?

Something they cannot even articulate?

People do not spend hard-earned dollars on products or services. They spend money to achieve an outcome.

If it really is all about them, you must know the result they expect and work backward from there.

Understanding the real value you deliver matters more than almost anything else in business.

So here is a quick test:

Ask yourself, "What business are we in?"

If your answer is:

"We fix gutters."

"We sell flowers."

"We clean pools."

"We do HVAC work."

"We sell sandwiches."

"We supply manufacturers."

"We build apps."

"We are food photographers."

"We teach dance."

Then you still have work to do.

Those are tasks. Not businesses. Not value. Not purpose.

Businesses built on tasks compete on price. Businesses built on purpose compete on meaning. That difference shows up directly on your bottom line. Sometimes in a very big way.

S2L: If your customer sees you as a commodity, you have already entered a race to the bottom. And unfortunately, you may already be on your way to winning it.

#11 BUY INTO THE NOT-SO-OBVIOUS: NARROWER GETS YOU WIDER.

"Perfection is achieved, not when there is nothing more to add, but when there is nothing left to take away." — *Antoine de Saint-Exupéry*

Most people are convinced that the wider the net, the bigger the catch. In business, that's almost never true...unless your company's name happens to be Amazon.

"Narrower gets you wider" is a mantra wired deep into my business DNA. The first time I heard that simple four-word statement from an internationally recognized sales trainer, I was convinced he was speaking gibberish. Turns out, he was voicing gospel. This is one of the most important, and most counterintuitive, concepts you'll find in this book.

It's natural to want to sell more things to more people.

It just feels like that should be the path to growth. But the truth? It's usually the path to confusion, dilution, and mediocrity.

I know a little something about fast food, having been the youngest franchisee in Burger King history back when BK was at its peak and new franchises were almost impossible to come by. I was all in...participating in regional marketing committees with Mad Men-style ad agencies in NYC, running Whopper boards at one of my six stores, scouting new locations. Not sure I loved it, but I lived it. To the tune of piling up business debt that even today would scare most of you reading this book.

And from that vantage point, I watched the industry's vaunted leader, McDonald's, pile almost everything except Pad Thai onto their menu. In their quest to be everything to everyone, they became less great at the things that made them great in the first place.

Then along came an obsessed young entrepreneur from Louisiana named Todd Graves, who thought he could build a fast-food empire by selling one thing: chicken tenders.

Bankers laughed. Guys like me, on the front lines of the Fast Food Wars, said, "No shot." We were all wrong. Dead wrong.

As McDonald's kept adding menu items, their customers grew confused, their marketing dollars became diluted, their employees got overwhelmed, and their customers got underwhelmed. Most importantly, real sales growth was quietly slipping out the back door.

Meanwhile, Todd's Raising Cane's sales were exploding.

Today, the average Raising Cane's unit is doing almost 150% of McDonald's sales. All while selling one primary item. Why?

Because they know their sweet spot. Because they execute with fanatical consistency. And because they do one thing ridiculously well. Mediocrity never ever makes the menu...for their customers or for their employees.

Todd Graves has long credited another master of the craft, In-N-Out Burger, whose menu has remained almost unchanged since 1948. Four items. Four. And they're still a juggernaut of epic proportions and the must-stop burger option if you're anywhere within 20 miles of a building bearing their highly recognizable sign.

But what about Costco, you say? Sure. Costco can sell copy machines and pretzel nuggets in the same aisle and get away with it. But they're an anomaly. And you'll go broke trying to follow their blueprint to sales.

Most customers, including you, want a provider who is exceptional at something, not okay at everything. Our 27-year-old daughter isn't looking for a mani-pedi from the staff that makes her protein smoothies. You're probably not excited about ordering sushi at your favorite Irish pub. And nobody's rushing to buy tires for their commercial van from the same shop that wrapped it with their logo last week.

Could you stretch a little beyond your lane? Absolutely. But stretch wisely. And never at the expense of what you do best.

S2L: Better is way better than more. And far more profitable. That's because "focus scales" and too often "sprawl fails."

#12 LEAN INTO YOUR USP.

You either have to be first, best, or different." —*Loretta Lynn*

That quote from the late country legend should become music to your ears.

Your company possesses a USP. A Unique Selling Proposition. Or at least I hope it does.

There is a reason you feel confident in what your company offers. Maybe you have a renowned chef, a patented process, unmatched service expertise, or access to leading-edge technology.

The list of potential advantages is long. But here is the hard truth. None of it matters unless it translates into greater customer satisfaction.

Your USP must be unmistakable to the customers you want to attract. It must be woven into the fabric of your company...how you sell, how you serve, how you hire, and how you communicate.

Ideally, you knew what made your business special before you opened your doors. Even so, I am still shocked when owners tell me there is almost no difference between them and their competitors.

If that's true, at best, the market will treat you exactly the same.

Wide receivers in football talk constantly about creating separation. Literally gaining space between themselves and the defender who is trying to stay glued to them. That is the only way that they can achieve success.

Business is no different.

So ask yourself:

- What truly separates us from our competition?
- What do we deliver that makes a customer's day, business, or life meaningfully better?
- What would customers miss immediately if we were gone tomorrow?

If those answers aren't clear, neither is your USP.

You and your team must live and breathe that advantage. Your prospects should understand it before the sale and feel it long after the transaction.

One important note.

If your only differentiator is being the lowest-priced option, that had better be because you possess a real and sustainable cost advantage in producing or acquiring what you sell.

Otherwise, that strategy almost always ends the same way:

- Margin erosion
- Brand dilution
- Customer disloyalty
- Financial stress

And yes...we will go much deeper into the art and science of pricing in the chapters ahead.

S2L: What you do best should never be a secret. Not to

your employees. Not to your customers. And certainly not to you. A USP that is clear, communicated, and consistently delivered is an all-important profit driver.

#13 BENEFIT FROM YOUR UNIQUENESS.

"You've got to have a competitive advantage — and you've got to know what it is." —*Jack Welch*

By now, you should be thinking far more critically about what actually sets you apart through the eyes of the most important person in your company's universe: the customer who chooses to buy what you sell.

One thing is certain.

It's called a *Unique* Selling Proposition for a reason.

Knowing what makes you different is important. *But uniqueness only becomes valuable when it is intentionally leveraged.*

Here's a real example worth sharing:

I've had the incredible privilege of working with a respected, family-owned RV dealership.

For those unfamiliar with the RV industry, Camping World, with its scale, buying power, and national footprint, has spent years buying out or squeezing out exactly the type of dealership I've consulted with these last four years.

From the minute I joined their efforts, my client and I knew that their survival and, more importantly, their ever-improving success were never going to hinge on price. Or selection. Or advertising spend.

It would hinge entirely on leaning in to their USP.

What would have seemed like their weakness to outsiders quickly became their advantage. The irony was striking.

Exploiting what many others likely assumed made them vulnerable...being small and locally owned...turned out to be their greatest strength.

With focus and discipline, they went all-in on what made them genuinely different. They positioned themselves clearly and consistently as the region's "trusted, family-owned RV partner."

A place where:

• Transparency wasn't a slogan, but rather standard practice.
• Questions were welcomed, not rushed.
• Concerns were addressed promptly.
• Customers worked with a dedicated, stable team, not a revolving door of inexperienced people simply there to collect a check.

That is real separation.

Do you know how difficult it is for a national corporation with 200+ locations across 46 states and well-documented employee retention challenges to deliver that level of personalized service?

It's nearly impossible.

Scale is powerful. But it often comes at the expense of intimacy, consistency, and trust.

Those incredibly skilled and committed business owners I have the privilege of working with leaned into what they could do better while never apologizing for what they couldn't. Today, they fully embrace being:

• Small

- Local
- Nimble
- Humble
- Customer-centric

The result? Consistent wins for them. Because they create consistent wins for their customers

Their uniqueness is no longer just a differentiator. It's their strategic advantage that continues to pay real dividends.

Are you truly exploiting your company's USP or merely acknowledging that it exists? There is a real, discernible difference.

S2L: Put a deliberate plan in place to turn your USP into a stronger bottom line. Then execute it relentlessly. Make your uniqueness a cornerstone of your profit strategy.

#14 BE BOLD!

"What would you do if you weren't afraid?" —*Sheryl Sandberg*

In competitive markets, playing it safe is rarely rewarded. So why then do so many small- to mid-size companies play it so safely? It's hard to win if you are always playing not to lose.

Boldness does not mean going for broke. It means making deliberate, well-informed decisions with conviction and then standing firmly behind them. Businesses that refuse to take that step rarely separate from the pack.

Now that you are getting to know me, you have probably realized I am certainly not allergic to bold. Quite the opposite. Need more proof?

When Roy Boe, the founder of the New York Islanders and the New York Nets, handpicked me to help launch a new American Hockey League team in Worcester, Massachusetts, challenges came with the territory. Roy had very little experience with AAA minor league sports and had largely ignored the fact that every professional sports franchise that had previously chosen Worcester had failed.

That made sense. Until then, Roy had been focused on

chasing Stanley Cups and NBA championships. Living an hour and a half away in affluent Fairfield County, Connecticut, he would be the first to admit he did not have a real pulse on Worcester.

That reality did not make my first month as Executive Vice President and minority partner especially smooth.

Just days in, Roy asked me what my top three priorities would be. He nearly fell over when I told him we would endeavor to build a fun, unmistakable, and bold brand, develop a one-of-a-kind Kids' Club, and create a legendary mascot.

"I thought we were in the hockey business," he said.

That was my cue to explain that we were in the *HockeyPlus* business. Big-time professional hockey combined with an interactive experience built for excitement and fun. We would be the entertainment alternative for families, not just hardcore sports fans. And yes, that is because I had done my homework on what makes AAA sports teams thrive.

To his credit, Roy gave me the room to run. With the right partners, a hard-working front office, and an outstanding partnership with the St. Louis Blues, we set Worcester on fire. Being bold took courage. On Roy's part. And mine.

Bold thinking has also become an absolute necessity in the restaurant world.

One of my favorite consulting clients was a two-partner restaurant group that had enjoyed steady success for decades. They had mastered the traditional lunch-and-dinner model. Then they landed an A-plus creekside location with a rent factor that would have scared away almost anyone. But them.

Instead of playing it safe, they chose to change the narrative.

We agreed they were not opening just another restaurant. They were creating *the* place to go. My team and I built a logo and tagline that reinforced that mission. As did the initial menu we arrived at.

They believed in their assets. A location that appealed to families and businesspeople, seniors and social crowds. A place where you could watch boats and dolphins coexist while enjoying a cold beer and great appetizers. They trusted their ability to deliver consistent food and drinks at prices that attracted customers rather than repelled them. And they were confident that once people came, they would return.

Fast forward eight years. They exceeded even their most optimistic expectations. And those expectations were pretty lofty.

They understood they were selling far more than fried seafood, outrageous appetizers, and tropical drinks inspired by a Bahamian tiki hut. They were selling fresh air. Nature. Community. Sunday afternoon boat getaways. Watercraft welcome, but not required. All at prices that said, "Come anytime."

It should not surprise you that they built indoor and outdoor bars, seating nooks throughout, sail-covered tables, standing areas to relax, and, yes, even a traditional dining room.

There is a lot to learn from a place that proudly features Trash Can Nachos as a signature item. They never forget why customers come. And why their bottom line continues to grow.

Ready to get bolder yet?

S2L: The entrepreneurs who separate themselves lead from the front. They take bold action, not reckless chances...well-calculated risks that create momentum others never achieve.

#15 RECOGNIZE YOUR COMPETITION.

"The sport of business is the ultimate competition. It's 7 × 24 × 365 × forever." —*Mark Cuban*

I cannot tell you how many times I hear prospective clients say, "No one is doing what we're doing." Honestly, I hear it far too often.

I appreciate the excitement. I respect the confidence. But c'mon, let's take the blinders off.

Maybe you are the only Mexican restaurant in town. You are still competing for the same food dollar as the pizza place down the road or the grocery store running a big taco night promotion on aisle three.

Maybe your software platform truly is first to market. Even so, the problem you solve has been handled somehow until now. And while you are celebrating your uniqueness, a well-funded competitor is already reverse engineering your idea and preparing to out-feature or undercut you just as you think you have crossed the minimum adoption threshold.

And yes, you might be the only optician in your small town. But you are also competing with a dozen online eyewear retailers who can deliver directly to your customers' doors within forty-eight hours.

I could go on, but you get the point.

You cannot build a successful business while wearing sunglasses in the dark. Even if you are that optician.

Do not pretend competition does not exist. Face it. Learn from it. Outwork it. Win by delivering on your promise with greater consistency and care than anyone else, every single day.

S2L: If you want to win, you must give customers clear reasons to choose you...and not your competitor.

#16 CREATE AWE.

"When you focus on people over profit, you end up being more profitable." —*Will Guidara*

Whether you're launching your first product or entering year twelve, the mission stays the same: Don't be awed. Generate awe, instead.

Awe your customer. Awe your client. Awe your consumer. Awe your follower.

How can a South Carolina tire company continue to build awe as it has done since it changed its first tire more than 50 years ago? Their female customers always find a rose on their front seat after their service is complete. That small, thoughtful gesture reinforces the idea that awe can be generated in an endless array of ways.

It's your job to make them want to come back. Whether you're a retailer, wholesaler, manufacturer, or service provider.

Make them want to tell their friends.

Make them proud to post about you without being asked.

If you've done your homework...really done it...you know your offer, your price, your delivery, and your entire buyer journey aren't just acceptable. They're irresistible. They leave people feeling more than satisfied. They leave them with a positive emotional aftertaste.

How do you know you've delivered awe?

The numbers always whisper or, better still, yell out the truth. Sometimes even immediately.

Customer count. Repeat rate. Referral traffic. Likes. Shares. Unsubscribes. Cart abandonment. Too many entrepreneurs ignore the very scoreboard built to show them exactly how they're performing.

S2L: Mediocrity never maximizes profits. But it always improves your chances of disappearing.

#17 CHALLENGE EVERYTHING YOU CURRENTLY DO.

"The first principle is that you must not fool yourself, and you are the easiest person to fool." —*Richard Feynman*

Many entrepreneurs I meet assume there are simple, clear-cut answers to the questions every business must wrestle with, whether they're running a startup or a family-owned legacy company. Well, they're fooling themselves.

Why? Because if you go back to Rule #1, you'll remember that the answers to the most basic business questions don't come from you; *they come from your customer.* And they change over time.

Continually ask yourself the questions that never go away.

- What exactly are we selling...and to whom?
- Why would they want to buy it at all?
- Why would they choose us instead of a competitor?
- What is the *right* price for them, not for us?
- Do *when*, *where*, and *how* meaningfully affect their buying decision?
- What can our team do to delight them...and motivate them to share our story?

• What is the best use of our time and capital *right now*?

These are not startup questions. They are survival questions.

In practice, what does that mean exactly? It means you never get to stop learning.

These questions demand that you understand, deeply and continuously, your customer's:

• Needs
• Desires
• Frustrations
• Trade-offs
• Willingness to pay
• Willingness to wait
• Willingness to travel
• Willingness to switch

Assumptions are dangerous. Confidence without evidence is fatal. And the market is brutally honest.

Need a wake-up call? Multiple reputable studies confirm that around 40 percent of small businesses fail because even though the entrepreneur believes there is real need and real demand for what they offer, the market disagrees. One thing is certain beyond a doubt. The customer always gets the final vote.

I hope it's clear now that *"Ready. Sell. Research." is a blueprint for struggle*, if not, total failure.

There is only one path that scales, and it looks like this:

Research. Plan. Sell. Listen. Refine. Sell. Listen. Refine. Sell. Repeat.

Repeating it often enough makes your success far less accidental. Because that's not a sign of hesitation or weakness. It is an ongoing example of discipline at work.

S2L: The sooner you accept that the customer is your boss, the faster your thinking shifts. And your results

lift. Without truly understanding what drives your customer, your profitability can't grow in a meaningful, sustainable way.

SECTION 3

Revisit How Profit Really Works.

#18 LISTEN TO THEIR BUYING HABITS.

"People vote with their dollars." —Thomas Sowell

Listen hard. Your customers are constantly telling *you* what matters most to *them*.

They're just not using words.

They speak through behavior. Through timing. Through frequency. Through what they buy, what they don't, and how often they come back for more. Yet far too many business owners never truly listen.

Most entrepreneurs believe they understand their customers because they talk to them. Conversations help. But buying habits tell the truth.

Your customer's spending patterns reveal:

- what they value
- what they trust
- what they ignore
- what confuses them
- what delights them

And they do it far more honestly than surveys or focus groups ever could.

Here's the problem. Many businesses look at sales in the aggregate. Monthly totals. Quarterly growth. Year-over-year comparisons. Those numbers matter, but they hide the details that actually drive profit.

Listening to buying habits requires curiosity and discipline. It means asking better questions of your data.

What sells consistently, and what spikes only when discounted?

What items are purchased together?

What days, times, or seasons matter most?

What products or services bring customers back again and again?

What do first-time buyers choose versus longtime customers?

Patterns always exist. The question is whether you are paying attention.

Customers vote with their wallets. Every purchase is a decision. Every repeat purchase is a signal. Every abandoned cart, returned item, or ignored upsell is feedback.

Too many businesses guess what customers want next instead of observing what they already want now.

Listening also means recognizing change early. Buying habits that shift before financial statements do. A slight dip in frequency. A change in product mix. A move toward lower-priced options. These are early warning signs, not random noise.

Entrepreneurs who listen closely can adjust before problems become painful. Those who don't often react too late.

This concept applies everywhere. Retail. Restaurants. Service businesses. Manufacturing. B2B. B2C. The principles don't change. Only the data does.

If you want to grow profitably, stop asking customers what they think and start observing what they do.

Their habits already contain the answers you're looking for.

S2L: Your customers always tell you the truth. The question is whether you are listening closely enough to hear it. Without listening attentively, you are very far from maximizing your bottom line.

#19 HEAR WHAT THE NUMBERS ARE SAYING.

"If you don't know your numbers, you don't know what's going on in your business." —*Marcus Lemonis*

As you move through this part of the book, one theme will become crystal-clear: knowing, understanding, and responding to "your numbers" isn't optional... It's foundational. And no numbers matter more than what you sell, how much of it you sell (your product mix), at what price, and at what time.

You'd assume everyone pays attention to those key metrics. But, they don't. Many entrepreneurs never study their product mix by the month—let alone by the day, the daypart, the week, or even the time of year. And that's just the starting point of meaningful product-mix analysis.

When I was a Burger King franchisee, I discovered quickly that Whopper Jr. sales had a bizarre yet undeniable correlation to restroom cleanliness. When female customers were put off by a dirty bathroom, their reaction showed up in the numbers: falling sales of their favorite menu item. Why? Because they stopped coming to that location altogether. The product mix revealed the story without one word being said.

Are you paying that level of attention to what your customers' spending habits are telling you? They speak loudest with their dollars. And today, with industry-specific software and powerful AI tools, there is no excuse for not knowing...down to the smallest detail...how your customers are responding.

S2L: The more you know about what they're buying, when they're buying, and how they're buying, the greater your odds of long-term success.

#20 MINE THE GOLD IN YOUR PRODUCT MIX NUMBERS.

"Every sale has five basic obstacles: no need, no money, no hurry, no desire, no trust." —*Zig Ziglar*

You can't overcome those five obstacles if you don't even know they're at play.

Why are sales up? Why are they down? Why are some products taking off online while others sit untouched? Why do sales surge when the weather turns bad? Why did customers stop ordering your best steak? Why do subscriptions crash after 90 days?

If you're not analyzing your sales numbers in multiple meaningful ways, you will fall well short of your true potential.

Do you know that your pink T-shirts barely move in extra large? Have you noticed that on game nights your bar fills with Bud drinkers, not craft beer buyers? Are you aware that every time you discount deeply, sales collapse when you return to full price? Have you checked whether a competitor's coupon drop is behind your sudden dip? Are you really sure sales improve when it snows? Have you compared online results based on where items are positioned on your site? Do you realize your top showerhead sells well, but only to a handful of contractors?

I could go on for pages, but the message is straightforward. You must mine your product mix carefully and consistently so you can respond quickly and adjust wisely. No excuses. It's worth repeating. With the software and AI tools available to you today, understanding these patterns has never been easier.

S2L: Dig deeper. Profit more.

#21 GUIDE THEM TO DELIGHT.

"If I had asked people what they wanted, they would have said faster horses." —*Henry Ford*

Talk about counterintuitive. You may be thinking, "I thought you wanted the customer to buy what they wanted?" Yes. And no. The goal is for the customer to walk away with the highest level of satisfaction possible. You still have significant influence over whether that happens.

If your research confirms that customers would love something they haven't yet bought, you absolutely have the ability to guide them toward it. A buyer couldn't have wanted a Model T before the Model T existed. Innovation often reveals desire, not the other way around.

It's our job to help customers understand what we know will satisfy them most. And it's our job to monitor whether that satisfaction is actually occurring. When it isn't, we have plenty of levers to pull to change the narrative. But that takes awareness, flexibility, and execution.

It may require updating your marketing, sales, and messaging strategy. You may need to rewrite your menu or reposition products on your website. And you will definitely need to re-educate and remotivate your team.

Let's dig a little deeper into this concept. It's that important.

S2L: Allowing customers to settle for something less than what's best for them lowers your odds of maximum short- and long-term success.

#22 BE CAREFUL NOT TO SCREW UP WHAT THEY ARE BUYING.

"If you want to grow your business, you must first understand your client's reality." —*Jay Abraham*

Smart business owners do their homework. They know exactly which level of service or tier of product will truly awe their prospective or current customers.

So why do so many businesses still steer buyers toward the wrong products for them?

Some of it comes from how we price. Some comes from how we reward salespeople or managers for the wrong sale. Some comes from flawed advertising. And much of it comes from how we present the choices in the first place.

Imagine you offer a multi-tier online platform. You know the lowest-priced plan will leave customers frustrated, but you only give them two options, and they keep choosing the cheap one. Research shows that when you add a premium third option, most customers choose the middle tier—the one you wanted them to buy all along.

We've already agreed that you want customers buying the best version of you because it will delight them the most. So tell them that. And then sell them that.

They should be flocking to that incredible new swimsuit you launched last week, but you photographed it poorly, priced it wrong, and buried it on your site and in your stores. How does that even happen?

One of my clients learned this lesson the hard way. Before hiring me, he was bonusing his restaurant manager for lowering the percentage food cost. That's the opposite of customer-centric. Because large fries carried a slightly higher percentage food cost, the manager pushed every customer toward small fries. But the customer wanted the large fries. They would have received a better value, and the owner would have made more penny profit and had a happier customer.

NOTE: We will discuss penny profit in depth shortly.

Need another real-life example? A highly successful high-volume restaurant client of mine was stunned when my product mix analysis revealed that five well-regarded bottles of wine were barely moving by the glass or the bottle. They were selling so slowly that a glass poured on Saturday often came from a bottle opened the previous Saturday. How could that possibly be acceptable? The restaurant expected better. Its customers expected better. The numbers were screaming for attention, but like so many busy operations, this one simply missed what was hiding in plain sight. They quickly responded and replaced those slow-selling alternatives with five that proved to move much faster.

Are you doing everything possible to ensure that what your customers are purchasing will lead to maximum satisfaction? Because a raving buyer returns...and refers.

S2L: Unintentionally leading your buyers to the wrong products is never good for your long-term bottom line.

#23 FORGET THE WAY YOU PROBABLY LOOK AT PRICING.

"Pricing is a marketing decision, not an accounting decision." —*Ron Baker*

Decades ago, when I was overloaded with economics courses at Wharton, nothing struck me more than the way I was taught the concept of pricing. To this day, I believe pricing remains one of the most important yet most *misunderstood* elements in all of business.

Whenever I discuss pricing with a client, their first instinct is always the same. They talk at length about their cost of producing the product or delivering the service. And the moment that I tell them that cost has very little to do with final price, their expression shifts to disbelief and confusion. Yet it's true when you understand the concept correctly.

As a consumer, do you know or care what it costs to build a new 36-foot diesel pusher Class A motorhome? And what does "cost" even mean? The chassis? The components? The labor and overhead?

As a business owner, do you know what it took to build QuickBooks or what it costs to maintain? Do you care? Nope.

Nope. Nope. And nope. Do their actual costs influence your decision to pay for their platform? Not at all.

Price is driven entirely by the value the buyer assigns to the offering.

So what is the real pricing equation?

The right price is the maximum amount a buyer will pay while still feeling satisfied and ideally delighted.

That's it. Period.

Before you rush to disagree, remember that your customer does not operate in a vacuum. Their sense of value is absolutely shaped, in part, by market expectations, competitor comparisons, the economy, and their own experiences.

S2L: An open mind about pricing strategy opens the door to stronger net revenue over the long term.

#24 ADJUST WHEN PRICE FAILS.

"Value is a perception, not a calculation." —*Rory Sutherland*

I've been doing this a long time. I can already hear the pushback: "What the customer wants to pay is way too close to my cost. What then?"

Then *you have four options.*

#1. Accept that you may not have a viable market for this product or service right now.

It happens. Not every idea has a ready audience at the price point you need.

#2. Do everything possible to meaningfully reduce your cost.

Cut waste, renegotiate, streamline, rethink the model.

#3. Work aggressively to increase their perception of value.

Value can be shaped through presentation, positioning, packaging, experience, and messaging.

#4. Acknowledge that some offerings may need to serve as loss leaders.

A loss leader is a product with little margin, no margin, or even negative margin that helps you make money elsewhere.

Your customer votes with their dollars. They understand

their alternatives. They're not naive, and in most cases they're realistic. You'll learn quickly what the maximum price is that still leaves them delighted.

S2L: Wasted energy costs money. Know what price will make your customer feel good before you get too deep into the launch of any new product, product line, or service offering.

#25 DON'T TRADE HIGHER PRICES FOR CUSTOMERS.

"Only the paranoid survive." —*Andy Grove*

As a franchisee, I learned quickly that my franchisor was obsessed with volume. Their revenue came from a percentage of top-line sales. We were regularly reminded that raising prices might cost customers and that this was simply an acceptable part of the franchisor's business model.

Let that sink in.

Raise prices. Lose customers.

What a brilliant strategy for long-term profitability, right?

It didn't work when I was a franchisee. And it rarely works now. Because a steadily shrinking customer count is almost always a warning sign that trouble is coming. At some point, there won't be enough customers left to raise prices on.

Are you spending as much time analyzing your customer counts as you are your total revenue? If not, that might be an exercise worth starting no later than tomorrow afternoon.

S2L: Increased revenue can trick you into believing everything is fine. Delve deeper.

#26 AVOID UNDERPRICING.

"Your customer's opinion is your reality." —*Warren Buffett*

Ready for another counterintuitive truth? *You can destroy your value perception by pricing your product or service too low.* Yes, too low.

Take Infiniti, Nissan's luxury brand. Its U.S. launch in 1989 is now a case study in ineffective pricing strategy. Infiniti was built to compete with Mercedes, Audi, Cadillac, and BMW, yet its pricing came in well below that tier. Instead of perceiving Infiniti as a value-driven luxury competitor during its launch, consumers immediately read the lower price as *a signal that the brand was inferior*. Like virtually all customers, luxury buyers vote with their wallets and their expectations. When the price sits outside the luxury orbit, they assume the quality sits outside it, too.

Infiniti eventually corrected course with a significant price increase, but much of the damage was done. Even worse...their long-term sales issues had less to do with price and everything to do with how the brand made buyers feel after the purchase.

They forgot the kid-glove follow-up and service that luxury buyers expect. Value perception cuts both ways.

Want an even more relatable example? Years ago, when I was running an American Hockey League team, our founder refused to eat at any restaurant that priced a 12-ounce sirloin or piece of fresh-caught swordfish under $30. Why? Because, like many buyers, he used price as a proxy for quality and freshness. Whether you admit it or not, you probably do the same.

Ever shopped at Erewhon in Los Angeles? Wealthy consumers walk out wearing an $80 Erewhon cap, carrying a $50 bottle of chicken soup in a $138 tote bag... and they feel great about it. Why? Because the *experience*, the *brand,* and the *perceived quality* justify the premium. They aren't buying soup. They're buying status, wellness, exclusivity, and identity.

Price matters in both directions.

Ask yourself honestly: would a new scent from Selena Gomez feel like a luxury fragrance if it were priced at $12.95? Of course not. The price would undermine the story.

Smart pricing doesn't cheapen your offering. *Smart pricing reinforces your value.*

S2L: Figure out how to build, package, and deliver your product or service so effectively that your customer feels even better when they pay more.

#27 MASTER YOUR COSTS.

"You can't afford to be unaware of your costs." —*Harvey Mackay*

Now that we've opened the door to understanding your costs, it's time to shift your mindset into high gear. Guessing at your costs isn't sloppy. It's dangerous. Too often it's the business equivalent of signing your own death certificate.

One moment from my career still stands out as if it happened yesterday. I was serving as President of an NBA D-League team in its second year, sitting in a small meeting room in a Charlotte hotel with the seven other Team Presidents, the NBA's lead attorney and NBA Commissioner David Stern, one of the most respected leaders in sports history. Each of us was about to face a single direct question from the Commissioner. My friend and fellow Team President to my left went first. Stern reminded him that his team and arena had been hand selected to host a major NBA preseason event. Then he asked, firmly, clearly and with zero room for escape:

"Exactly how many tickets do you need to sell for us to break even?"

My friend answered quickly. "I think..."

Mr. Stern abruptly cut him off. "'I think' is not a number." Then he asked the exact same question, this time with even greater precision.

My friend tried again. "Well..."

The Commissioner stopped him a second time. "Neither is 'well.' You have all my contact information. When you have the actual number that you should have already known, call me."

The room went silent. And I mean silent. The truth? Most of us in that room that day couldn't have answered a similar numbers-related question to Commissioner Stern's standards. And that was a problem. A big one.

It was a lesson I never forgot.

But this book isn't about me, the world's premier basketball league or Commissioner Stern. It's about you and the absolute necessity of knowing your costs with precision, not approximation. It's about your business. So ask yourself:

Do you fully grasp both your fixed costs and your variable costs? Do you realize that thoroughly understanding the clear difference between the two, and how they interact, is essential to profitability and long-term growth? Do you need to be reminded that it is simply impossible to determine any breakeven points or to make any sound decisions about pricing, staffing, capacity, and growth without that awareness?

How well do you know your exact sales numbers? Are you cognizant of any increases in your raw costs? Are you ignoring your soft costs without even realizing it?

How fast can you access the numbers that matter? And how often do you adjust your behavior based on what those numbers are telling you?

If you don't know these answers cold, you're running blind. And blind businesses ultimately have a tough time seeing long-term success.

S2L: Never forget. "I think" is not a number. And it's not data you can build a profitable business on.

#28 GET REAL REGARDING YOUR IDEAL COSTS.

"Thinking something does not make it true. Wanting something does not make it real." – *Michelle Hodkin*

Please sit up in your chair for this one. It matters.

When we build business plans and pro formas, we start by identifying what we believe each product costs to make. We see the invoices. We know the ingredients. We understand the formulas. On paper, costing things out feels straightforward.

So if we add up the cost of the 27 components used to manufacture a diaper at a plant where I was brought in to consult, we should know our cost of goods. Right?

Yes. And no.

What we have identified is the *ideal cost*. From there, we project profitability based on our cost of goods. Everything looks clean and comforting.

But ideal costs live in a perfect world. The real world is far messier.

A component breaks or arrives flawed.

A shipment is crushed and requires a rush replacement.

Inventory walks out the back door.

A conveyor is fed incorrectly and a full batch is ruined.

Those circumstances define your *real cost*.

In food and beverage, the gap is often even wider. A steak hits the floor. Drinks go on the house. Product spoils. One employee consistently overportions because it "looks better."

You already know this story. The real question is how you recognize and measure the gap between ideal and real.

In that diaper plant, we carefully calculated ideal costs, then compared them to actual inventory usage and product mix data to determine real costs. The variance was significant. It explained exactly why projected profits never materialized.

Even if you are only reselling finished goods, the problem does not go away. Shrinkage, damage, and other losses still widen the gap between what should happen and what actually does.

Once this foundational ideal versus real concept clicks, you will see that it applies to labor costs as well. You can project what a cashier, a landscaper, or even a software engineer should produce. But the odds that those assumptions align with actual hourly, daily, or annual output are slim. Understanding why that gap exists, and what it takes to reduce it, is essential to sustained profitability.

The good news is that technology now makes identifying, measuring, and closing these gaps far easier across nearly every industry.

S2L: Ideal conditions create false confidence. Real conditions determine profit.

#29 SHRINK THAT REAL VS. IDEAL GAP.

"...clarity is power." —*Yuval Noah Harari*

Yes...*ideal vs. real cost analysis software exists*. And it's often essential.

You may see it labeled as theoretical vs. actual, standard vs. actual, or expected vs. actual costing. The labels vary. The purpose does not.

These tools compare:

• the ideal...the recipe, plan, estimate, and best-case scenario
• to the real...What actually happened?

Then they expose the variance.

This software shows up in restaurant inventory platforms, manufacturing ERP systems, construction job-costing tools, and retail shrink dashboards. Different industries. Same problem.

The software exists for one reason: to show you exactly where money leaked out between the clean assumptions of your pro forma and the reality of daily operations.

Most companies can't afford not to use it.

The gap between ideal and real always exists. Smart businesses measure it. When you measure the gap, you can close it. And when you close it, profit improves immediately... without raising prices or adding sales.

The even better news: *affordable tech tools* now exist to assist you in analyzing ideal vs. real labor costs as well.

S2L: Identifying the gap is essential. Profitability improves only when you actively work to reduce it.

#30 RECOGNIZE THAT YOUR CHEAPEST OPTION MAY BE YOUR MOST EXPENSIVE.

"It's unwise to pay too much, but it's worse to pay too little." —*John Ruskin*

Maybe I should have titled this book *An Exercise in Counterintuitive Thinking*, because here we go again.

Most entrepreneurs are constantly looking for ways to save money. That instinct is natural. Cash is finite. Margins matter. Every dollar feels personal. So how can trying to save money that lies around every corner possibly be bad?

Well…it can be really bad. And often is.

That's because there is a critical difference between being *cost-conscious* and being *cost-driven*. One protects profitability. The second quietly erodes it. Or not so quietly.

The cheapest option almost always looks good in the moment. How could it not? It shows up nicely on a spreadsheet. It reduces upfront pain. It feels responsible. And it's often exactly what your accountant or your buddies encourage. "Why pay more?"

But as I remind my clients regularly, it's not what you pay. It's what you get.

When Dunkin' scouts a new location, they only consider

properties on the side of the street where morning traffic peaks. If a similar property across the road were available for half the price, or even free, they would pass. They understand something many business owners don't. Cheap rent is rarely cheap.

Inconvenient access, poor visibility, lack of foot traffic, or the wrong neighboring businesses can cost far more in lost sales and profit than you could ever save in monthly rent. The right storefront, the better industrial park, or the higher-profile office building often works to your advantage every single day. Ironically, cheaper locations often produce higher rent as a percentage of sales because revenue is capped.

I can already hear your question. What if we can't afford the better location? My response is very straightforward. "Will you be able to survive the inferior sales your inferior location will yield? Will you be able to weather what will actually turn out to be an even higher rent factor?"

The same logic applies to equipment purchases. Choosing the least expensive option often leads to:

- More downtime
- More repairs
- Shorter lifespan
- Higher replacement costs

You see, the true cost of equipment isn't its purchase price. It's its functionality. Its reliability. And its ability to grow with you. When equipment fails, your productivity stops, your customers wait, and your employees scramble. Oh yeah, then wait to see what that equipment is worth when you try to trade it in for what you should have bought in the first place.

Costco understood this principle decades ago when it came to labor. That's why you see their employees wearing badges that read "23 years of service" or "Proud team member since 2012." They learned early that cheap hires require more supervision, make more mistakes, frustrate customers more regularly, and often leave just as they are about to become marginally useful. That turnover has a real cost, even if it doesn't show up neatly in your accounting software. And that cost can quietly destroy your bottom line. That is why at Costco, they pay more, hire fewer, need less, and accomplish more.

Training is another place where entrepreneurs try to save and often pay dearly. Skipping or minimizing training doesn't just slow employees down. It sets them up to make decisions that damage customer trust and brand perception, both of which are long-term business killers.

The same trap exists with technology. Free or bargain tools look appealing until they don't integrate, don't scale, and/or don't support growth. When workarounds become the norm, you're already deep in the weeds.

Confusing price with cost is easy. But they are far from the same thing.

Price is what you pay today.

Cost is what it takes to fix, replace, manage, and recover tomorrow.

The cheapest option usually doesn't eliminate cost. It simply transfers it to places that are harder to measure and far more damaging long-term.

S2L: The lowest price rarely delivers the lowest cost, the smartest value, or the highest profit. Invest with a clear understanding of where failure would be most expensive. Your company's future depends on it.

#31 DISTINGUISH THE CRITICAL DIFFERENCE BETWEEN PENNY AND PERCENTAGE PROFIT.

"The problem with experts is not that they know too little, but that they know too much that isn't so." — *Nassim Nicholas Taleb*

Everybody loves great profit margins, right? And on the surface, margins seem simple enough. Except...they're not.

That's exactly why this section matters so much to me. As it should to you. Most business owners accept their accountant's logic without question. A 25% cost of goods must be better than a 30% cost of goods, right? How could it not be?

Well, get ready...because this may be the most counterintuitive concept in the entire book. After decades working with businesses of every shape and size, I've learned that we need to focus heavily on Profit Margin 101.

As an earlier chapter alluded to, *two completely different ways exist to look at margins when it comes to the cost of your goods or services.* Both are legitimate. Both matter. But they each tell a very different story.

1. Percentage Profit

Percentage profit expresses margin by looking at cost as a percentage of your selling price. Let's keep it simple:

You sell a plain cheese pizza for $10. Your cost is $4.
Under standard accounting principles:

- Cost of goods = 40%
- Gross margin = 60%

(And yes, this ignores labor, overhead, and all the other inputs, which explains why it's often called gross profit.) This is a metric CFOs love. But it's not the whole picture.

2. Penny Profit

Penny profit looks at the same transaction but through a far more practical lens: actual dollars earned.

You sell that same pizza for $10 that costs you $4.

Your penny profit is $6. Not a percentage. Not a ratio. Six real dollars you can actually put in the bank.

Many businesses...and many CFOs and most outsourced accounting firms...will rely exclusively on percentage profit as the measure of your success.

But making decisions on percentages alone can be a costly mistake. Don't be fooled into thinking that percentage profit is the absolute best barometer to measure your margins relating to your cost of goods.

Percentage tells you how something looks. Penny profit tells you how much money you actually make.

Understanding both will likely shift your mindset. For the better.

S2L: To maximize your bottom line, you must evaluate cost of goods in both percentages and dollars before pricing and promoting, as the examples ahead will make unmistakably clear.

#32 GET READY TO THINK
AND RESPOND DIFFERENTLY.

"Measurement is fabulous. Unless you're busy measuring what's easy to measure as opposed to what's important."
—*Seth Godin*

Everyone loves pizza, so let's start there.

At Pepe's Pizza Place, a plain cheese pizza sells for $10.

Food cost: $4

Percentage cost: 40% Percentage margin: 60%

Penny profit: $6

Pepe's House Special, loaded with every topping imaginable, sells for $16.

Food cost: $8

Percentage cost: 50% Percentage margin: 50%

Penny profit: $8

Now comes the million-dollar question: Which pizza would you rather sell?

Some of you are already thinking, *"Easy. Raise the House Special to $20 and match the margin."*

But remember Rule #1: What delights the customer?

Pepe's customers have already answered that question. They

love the House Special, but they simply can't justify paying twice the price of the plain pie.

So with that reality in mind, which pizza should Pepe push?

There is only one logical answer. The House Special, priced at $16, puts more actual dollars into his business...two extra dollars per sale. Those extra dollars pay for employees, rent, utilities, advertising, equipment, and everything else that keeps the lights on.

And there's more. The customer is happier. The House Special delivers more satisfaction, more perceived value, and more flavor.

So yes, this author is suggesting Pepe promote the House Special. All day. Every day.

Which raises an obvious question.

Why do so many accountants obsess over percentage cost of goods?

Because it feels obvious. Because it's easy to track. Because it fits neatly into a spreadsheet.

And because too many people confuse what is simple to measure with what actually matters.

How else do you explain a wildly successful smash-burger restaurant in California dropping its tater tots...not because customers didn't like them, but because they liked them too much?

The tots had a slightly higher percentage food cost than French fries. So management took them off the menu entirely.

Had they been looking at the world in pennies instead of percentages, simple pricing adjustments could have kept tater tots on the menu.

Instead, by eliminating a key differentiator, the restaurant was rewarded with hundreds of negative online comments, many from customers vowing that they would never return.

That decision didn't reduce cost. It transferred it...to lost loyalty, lost differentiation, and lost revenue.

The same misplaced thinking explains why a nationally

recognized chef-owner I knew personally instructed his servers to recommend the pasta over his highly regarded lobster dish.

His reasoning? The pasta had a wonderfully low 12% food cost. The lobster's percentage cost was nearly double.

Case closed. Or so he thought.

What he failed to realize...brace yourself...was that the lobster dish left diners in awe and still produced a penny profit greater than the entire menu price of the pasta.

Read that again. Slowly.

The only winners in that scenario were people who believe a lower food cost percentage is the Holy Grail. Unfortunately, it often is far from it.

That's because too many CFOs are convinced that a higher percentage margin automatically means a better bottom line.

Except it doesn't. Not always. And sometimes not even close.

In fact, percentage margin is occasionally the wrong metric to focus on at all. And an even worse one to build employee incentives around.

This way of thinking is not limited to restaurants.

The concept of penny profit applies across industries. It applies to product mix, service offerings, add-ons, equipment decisions, and yes...even labor costs, for those sophisticated enough to understand its nuances.

Because facts are facts. Customers don't buy percentages. Banks don't accept percentages.

And your business can't run on theoretical "better margins" that never translate into real dollars earned.

Penny profit tells the real story. *Penny profit fuels your business. Penny profit pays your bills.* And penny profit can fund your growth. And build your future.

S2L: Unless your bank lets you deposit percentages, follow the dollars. And follow your customers.

#33 ANTICIPATE PRICE RESPONSE.

"A business that doesn't understand its pricing doesn't understand its business." —*W. Edwards Deming*

By now, you might be starting to think that the old "mark it up until you hit your percentage margin goal" approach is, at best, off target. It's an approach that practically screams, "Customer? Oh... yeah, I forgot about them." Let's look at what this actually looks like in the wild.

You run a gourmet kitchen shop. You buy a high-end cappuccino machine for $209. Your CFO, or maybe your accountant, or both, insists your magic number is a 60% gross margin. So what do you do? You mark it up to $522.50.

Really? I can't tell you how often I've seen this tactic...and how often it backfires. So what's wrong with that strategy, you ask? A better question might be, "What's right with it?"

Let's revisit Rule #1: Your customer matters the most. By far. Not your spreadsheet. Not some theoretical margin target. Your customer. *What does it take to delight them?*

You're asking someone to spend the equivalent of a car payment on a machine that makes hot drinks. Does $522.50 feel like a "yes" price? Or does it feel like, "Let me think about that... forever"?

Now ask yourself, "What if you priced it at $495 instead?" A subtle change and unfortunately one that hurts your percentage profit. But...

- How many more units would you sell?
- How much happier would your customer be?
- How much more money would you put in your pocket...not in percentage terms, but in actual dollars?

Now you can really see the penny-profit vs. percentage-margin debate begin to kick in, yes?

And here's yet another kicker regarding price: If you believe that someone is willing to pay $522.50, do you really think they wouldn't stretch to $524.95 or even $525? That tiny jump is almost pure profit, yet it never gets considered because everyone is worshipping the percentage instead of the perceived value the customer assigns to it.

Pricing takes research and forethought. During my time helping ski resorts increase both lift-ticket and food-service revenue, I was asked to apply these same principles in one of the busiest on-mountain areas. Two quick stories from that assignment prove the point.

First, when I arrived, they had smartly priced items at $2.95 instead of $3.05 and $9.95 instead of $10.00—because they understood price perception. But then they made a simple mistake: they baked the 5% state tax into all their menu-board prices.

My recommendation?

Keep the prices customers already found fair and add the sales tax at checkout, just like every other retail transaction they'd participate in all week long.

The result? Zero complaints and an extra $100,000 to the bottom line in one season.

Sometimes fumbling with a few extra pennies is worth every penny.

Let's face it. Bean counters love margins. Me? I love exceeding customer expectations. You can chase perfect margins and impress your accountant. Or you can optimize actual dollars earned, sell more product, create happier customers, and send more profit to the bottom line.

I know which path I'm taking. And I have no problem teaching my CFO why. Or yours.

S2L: Remember. It's how you price, not how high you price, that drastically impacts the dollars you send to your bottom line. In both the short and long term.

#34 PRIORITIZE VALUE ADD.

"Value is defined by the buyer, not the seller." —*Alan Weiss*

Speaking of beans and bean counters... By pure good fortune, I discovered a wonderful French-style bistro in Hollywood recently where I ordered my infamous large, half-caf, breve iced latte. To my amazement, I watched the barista make it, add the ice, and then *can it* right in front of me.

Yes. *Can it*.

He handed me a clear plastic can with a sealed, easy-to-pop top. I was stunned by the presentation, yet pleasantly surprised that the price sat well within my normal "acceptable" range. His process was a textbook lesson in presentation, value-add, and penny profit-based pricing.

That can cost him $.95. He added only $1.00 to the price he had charged previously when serving the same drink in a standard disposable cold cup.

Let that sink in. He added virtually no markup at all on the can itself.

To anyone obsessed with percentage cost of goods, this

would have looked like a disaster. His cost-of-goods percentage just skyrocketed. But he wasn't thinking like an accountant. *He was thinking like a customer.*

He knew and was comfortable with the dollar margin he was already making on an iced latte. He kept that margin and added an extra dose of delight. And that delight was worth far more than a few extra percentage points on a spreadsheet. All raising the price would have done was scare customers away and kill the goodwill the can could have created.

His approach worked.

I literally walked past two other coffee shops every day on my West Coast trek to get that canned latte...and I almost always bought a cookie. Those were high-margin add-on sales that happened only because he had successfully implemented a simple, brilliant value-add.

I wasn't alone. Women heading to the gym next door were blown away by how convenient the can was to carry.

He created a new USP in one stroke. His toughest sell now? His accountant.

Because the more lattes he sells, the worse his percentage cost of goods looks. And the better his actual profit becomes. And the happier his customers are.

Let's go back to my time in the ski business. I wanted one of my clients to add a bacon cheeseburger to the menu. Skiers wanted more pizzazz than a simple cheeseburger offered. The challenge was that the round bacon we needed cost $.50, and they were used to operating with a strict 25% cost-of-goods target.

Four-timing the bacon cost made no sense. So we doubled it instead, adding only $1.00 to the traditional cheeseburger price.

Who won? Everyone. Except those seeking lower percentage food costs.

Customers loved the value. And we made more penny profit on every bacon cheeseburger sold.

It did not take much education for their astute CEO to comprehend that percentage metrics alone do not determine profitability. Sometimes, they actually hide it.

S2L: Combining value-add with penny-profit-focused pricing creates profit lifts that percentage thinking will never see.

SECTION 4

Run Your Business without Losing Control.

#35 STOP COMPLAINING ABOUT EMPLOYEE CHALLENGES. IMMEDIATELY.

"The way we treat our employees is the way they will treat our customers." —Howard Schultz

If you're like most companies, your people aren't part of your business. *They are your business.*

Every customer interaction...in person, online, on the phone, in the field...is shaped by an employee. Your server. Your installer. Your technician. Your driver. And yes, even if your company is online-only, your tech team is the reason your customers stay happy. Or don't.

Your creators...your chef, your bodywork specialist, your screen-printing manager...are the hands and minds behind the promise you've made to your customers? They define the quality you deliver.

So why do so many business owners treat employees as costs instead of assets? Why do we hire "positions" instead of hiring people?

You can have a fantastic product. You can run great-looking ads. Your online presence can kick butt. But try delivering excellence with a team that consistently falls short.

You won't. And your customers will let you know it in any variety of ways.

I already know the objections forming in your mind. "There just aren't enough good people to hire." Well, guess what? You chose to go into business.

It is your responsibility to:

- Find the right people.
- Train them well.
- Motivate them consistently.
- Reward them appropriately.

If you can't do that, your time as an entrepreneur will be short-lived. And honestly, that's how it should be.

Great employees don't cost you money. They make you money. High-performing employees are profit multipliers who...

- Catch issues early.
- Waste less.
- Manage time better.
- Own their outcomes.
- Improve efficiency.
- Reduce turnover, training, and customer churn.
- See problems you don't notice.
- Spot opportunities you don't have time to explore.
- Generate new ideas, better processes, and smarter solutions.

Poorly trained and disengaged employees, on the other hand, excel at only one thing. That is, standing between you and meaningful profitability. Sometimes they even help eliminate your profitability altogether. And why?

The answer goes back to Rule #1.

You are a customer dozens of times a week. You know instantly when you encounter a great employee versus one who underdelivers. And that difference directly determines where you spend your hard-earned dollars.

So why would it be any different for your own customers?

S2L: Your employees will determine how profitable your business can ultimately become.

#36 TREAT YOUR PEOPLE LIKE THEY'RE THE KEY TO YOUR PROFITABILITY.

"Employees are a company's greatest asset. They are your competitive advantage." —Anne Mulcahy

I have already drawn attention to Todd Graves, the founder of Raising Cane's, for focusing on doing one thing extremely well... chicken tenders. But he will be the first to tell you that their real success came from building one of the strongest restaurant cultures in America on three deceptively simple concepts. *Recognize. Respect. Reward.*

And he did not bury them in a training manual or throw a few posters on the wall. He built them into the way his company actually behaves. Those behaviors helped Raising Cane's grow faster, retain people longer, and boost and protect profitability at every stage.

#1. *People want to be seen.* Not with fifteen-dollar plastic plaques or a rah-rah speech at a year-end potluck dinner. They want to be recognized in the midst of the action... in front of their peers, their customers, their bosses. When someone quietly handles a tough customer. Or steps in for a teammate. Or turns a bad moment into a smooth one.

Todd Graves reminds us that recognition is invaluable, yet

costs you nothing. So why is that simple concept ignored by so many companies? Few things strengthen profitability more than free fuel for the behaviors you want repeated. When employees feel seen for doing the right things, they keep doing them. When they feel invisible, they stop caring, and your profit suffers long before you realize it.

You cannot build a profitable business on people who do not care.

#2. *Respect is not complicated.* It is how you talk to people. It is whether you give them the tools to succeed. It is whether you care enough to make schedules fair. It is whether you protect their dignity. And it is one of the easiest ways to reduce turnover...one of the most expensive drains on profitability.

But respect requires more than just talk. You see it in how leadership communicates. You see it in the tone they use with crew members. You see it in the decisions they make around hours, holidays, and business expectations. The more consistent the respect, the stronger the loyalty and the healthier the margins.

Respect is not something you teach or talk about. It is something you show. Over and over. Until your people truly believe you mean it. And then you keep showing it.

#3. *Even rewards do not have to be expensive.* They just have to be meaningful. Bonuses are great. Raises are great. But so are small wins. A surprise gift card. A note from a manager who paid attention. A moment of public appreciation. A chance to lead a shift early because the potential is there. A happy birthday message to an employee's spouse.

Todd never forgot what many leaders miss. *Rewards shape behavior. People repeat what gets rewarded. They stop what gets ignored.* Your profit margin often mirrors how consistently you reward the right things.

Reward the things that build your culture. Address the things that destroy it. Your company becomes whatever you shine the spotlight on, and your profitability follows that spotlight every single time.

Recognize. Respect. Reward. Repeat. Yes, repeat, because a lasting culture takes ongoing focus. Every day. For as long as you are in business. And if Todd and his team can make that happen with employees serving chicken tenders, you can certainly make it happen with employees feeding freshly cut branches into a wood chipper or folks feeding fabric into a pattern machine.

S2L: When your people feel recognized, they give more. When they feel respected, they stay longer. When they feel rewarded, they push harder. And when all three happen at once, your company will finally unlock its full profitability potential.

#37 NEVER FORGET RULE #1.

"Customer service shouldn't just be a department; it should be the entire company." —*Tony Hsieh*

Large banks spend ridiculous amounts of money trying to win your business. Ads. Fee waivers. Bundled services. Matched terms.

So why does a close friend of mine who has lived in Southern California for more than a decade stay loyal to a small New England bank? Because a real person answers the phone. No phone tree. No runaround.

Are those sentiments unique? Hardly.

When you initially opened this book, you almost immediately ran right into my not-so-subtle reminder that *your first responsibility as an entrepreneur is simple*: to meet and exceed the expectations of your customer.

Client. Consumer. Buyer. Patron. Whatever word you use, it's the same truth. *So why then do so many businesses behave as if their customer is an afterthought?*

Why do they believe that...

• Getting trapped in that phone tree is somehow OK?

- A script can replace a genuine conversation?
- Printing a smiley face on a receipt changes how a customer feels?
- "Customer service" belongs to one person or one department, instead of the entire organization?
- The customer is okay "rocking out" to endless on-hold music?
- Untrained, uninformed salespeople are acceptable?
- A current customer deserves less attention than a potential new one?"
- Low prices can magically erase a lousy experience?

Let's clear a few things up.

- Your logo doesn't answer questions.
- Your marketing doesn't fix problems.
- Your mission statement doesn't rescue bad moments.
- You cannot outspend a bad reputation.
- Poor service forces you to discount. Instead, focus on creating genuine connections with your customers. Building trust and providing exceptional service will not only enhance your reputation but also lead to long-lasting loyalty and repeat business. Great service lets you charge more.
- A delighted customer becomes free advertising. A frustrated customer becomes a virtual megaphone surrounded by online review sites eager to amplify their voice.
- Return customers cost less, buy more, and stay longer.
- Excellent service builds a moat around your business.

And when something goes wrong, the best companies don't disappear. Instead, they show up.

S2L: When customer focus drives every action you take, you multiply your odds of both short-term wins and long-term success.

#38 FORCE YOURSELF TO BE YOUR OWN CUSTOMER.

"There is only one boss. The customer." —*Sam Walton*

It's only natural to assume you understand what your customers feel. After all, odds are you built the business, chose the products or services, set the pricing, and shaped the experience.

But this fact is indisputable. Assuming what your customer feels is comfortable. Experiencing it can be humbling.

That's because *most leaders don't actually know what it feels like to be their customer.* They know what it feels like to be the boss. They go to the front of the line, skip the website, and bypass the processes associated with ordering, payment, and delivery. If you are like most owners, your people likely provide you with VIP treatment.

The most profitable businesses in the world share one trait. They build decisions around the actual customer experience, not the imagined one.

So let's be clear. If you want to grow both your top line and your bottom line, you must force yourself to be your own customer. Not once. Not occasionally. Relentlessly.

If you own a retail business, start paying attention the

moment you pull into the parking lot. Is it well lit? Is it clean? Is it welcoming? How long does it take to be greeted?

If you own a restaurant, see how quickly you receive a menu? Try ordering through DoorDash and evaluate the entire journey. If your presence might skew the experience, send a neighbor instead.

If you are an online merchant, experience the entire buyer's journey on your website. Including returning a product. Google your company. Measure how long your site takes to load. Place an order from start to finish, including payment and delivery setup. Try contacting customer support with a basic question.

Sign up for your own subscription. Order a refill. Schedule an appointment. Put yourself on your mailing list. Call after hours with a question.

Run a landscaping business? Have your team video the before and after of today's projects. Own a manufacturing plant? Invite a customer onto a Zoom call and give them permission to vent. Call your office from an unrecognized phone number and time how long you sit on hold.

You see where this is going.

When I was managing my first Burger King franchise, the company's district manager visited regularly to critique and evaluate. One day he taught me an invaluable lesson. He forced me to sit in the dining room facing both the counter and the drive-through window and simply observe.

The ground rules were clear. I was not allowed to get up, fix anything, address a bottleneck, or apologize to a customer.

When I asked why, his answer stuck with me. Because I could not possibly be there during every hour we were open, I needed to see my team and my systems operating without me.

Those early sessions were painful. Chained to a booth and forced to watch, I saw countless small failures. Service gaps. Missed steps. Low standards being quietly accepted.

Those observations taught me something numbers never could. The customer experiences everything. And you do not.

What I saw made something obvious. The gap between ideal service and actual execution was far too wide and appeared far too often. The solution then was the same as it is now. Identify the gaps. Prioritize them. Fix them fast.

Once you begin consistently shopping your own business, start shopping your competitors. Identify where you hold advantages and where they may be outperforming you.

But none of this matters if you fail to act.

Remove friction. Improve speed. Upgrade the experience. Train differently. Communicate better. Simplify the journey. Change what no longer works.

If buying from you would frustrate you, why would it delight your customers?

S2L: Experiencing your business the way your customers do is the fastest path to truth. And how can understanding the truth not be the fastest path to maximizing profitability?

#39 MASTER THE ONLY THREE WAYS TO GROW YOUR BUSINESS.

"It is not enough to do your best. You must know what to do, and then do your best." —*W. Edwards Deming*

If the above quote is true, why do so many entrepreneurs seem to consistently miss the boat? Could it be that they fail to realize that no matter how long they've been in business, their path to sales is built on just three levers? Only three. And they haven't changed for centuries. Literally.

Everything else is noise, distraction, or a symptom of these core drivers.

Those three levers are simple:

1. Get more people to try you.
2. Get the people who already buy from you to buy more often.
3. Increase the dollar amount of each customer transaction.

That's it. Every revenue problem, every stalled quarter, every disappointing year can be traced back to one, two, or all three.

Let's break them down.

1. Trial. Getting more people to experience you once.

Trial is the moment someone gives you a shot. Their first visit. First purchase. First appointment. Your first impression. Their first risk.

In today's digital world, *too many businesses chase attention instead of intention.* They look for viral moments instead of creatively sharing clear reasons for someone to walk through the door. And then proceed to checkout.

Trial grows when you make it easy for new customers to say yes and remove the friction that makes them hesitate.

People try you when:

- They believe you solve a problem they care about.
- Someone they trust recommends you.
- Your message is clear.
- Your offer feels safe, simple, or compelling.
- Your process is designed to eliminate uncertainty.

It's great to have a big sales funnel or an extensive sales pipeline. But there is no trial until they exchange dollars for what you offer. When you hear people talking about their CAC, or Customer Acquisition Cost, it is because they are in search of the expense they lay out to get one customer to try their product or service. That obviously matters. When it becomes clear that CAC is exceeding a customer's lifetime value, it is imperative to act quickly.

One thing is certain. You can't earn a regular customer without trial. Trial is the spark. Nothing grows without it.

2. Frequency. Getting customers to come back.

The most expensive thing you will ever do is acquire a new customer. By far, the most profitable thing you will ever do is keep one.

Frequency is the result of trust. It's the evidence that you delivered what you promised. It's your customer declaring, "I didn't just like that. I want more of it."

When customers return:

- Your marketing costs drop.
- Your revenue becomes predictable.
- Your margins expand.
- Your brand strengthens.
- Your operations stabilize.

Yet, way too many entrepreneurs focus their attention and dollars on trial. That's because too many entrepreneurs ignore the fact that frequency doesn't happen accidentally. *Frequency must be nurtured* intentionally. You earn it by delivering consistently, solving problems predictably, and making customers feel valued, understood, and remembered.

Why then have I been around so many clients who bonus their salespeople for landing a new customer and provide little or nothing to the salesperson for keeping an existing customer both engaged and satisfied?

In Pete's world, who is your most important customer? The one you already have. Treat them with so much reverence that a rival cannot duplicate how your customer feels when they're with you.

3. Average Check. Increasing the value of each transaction.

This can be where profit really lifts.

Average check is not about squeezing customers or jamming

some superfluous add-on down their throats. It's about serving them more completely. It's about offering solutions that enhance what they already came for.

People spend more when:

- You package value.
- You offer additional solutions.
- You educate instead of push.
- You make the buying decision smooth.
- You elevate their experience.

Raising the average check is not a financial trick. It's a service mindset.

Can you make your diner add dessert to their order tonight? Can you convince your software buyer to purchase the premium version? Can you get the clients whose lawn you cut to add summer and winter cleanup to the services they purchase? Can you get your retail client to buy the board shorts with the new polo shirt they are about to purchase?

Most importantly, can you do that by adding value without being pushy and a turnoff? The fact is that when you help customers achieve more, enjoy more, or avoid more pain, they willingly invest more.

Small increases when compounded over dozens, hundreds, or even thousands of transactions create massive results. Just a 10 percent increase in overall average check paired with even modest improvements in trial and frequency can transform a business that feels stuck in neutral into one that feels unstoppable.

So what should be the big takeaway? Every initiative, every campaign, every training, every system, and every tool should support at least one of these three levers.

Three levers. One shared goal. If it doesn't improve trial, frequency, or average check, your business won't grow. But remember: your customers do not want to be sold; they want to buy what gives them real value. By now, that should make complete sense.

S2L: Increasing revenue isn't complicated, really. Improve the number of people who try you, the number who return, and the value you deliver each time. Added profit will quickly follow.

#40 LEAD WITH CHANGE BEFORE BEING DRAGGED INTO IT.

"Companies rarely die from moving too fast, and they frequently die from moving too slowly." —*Reed Hastings*

Being comfortable is wonderful on a cold Saturday night, covered in blankets, watching Netflix with a hot cocoa in hand. *But being comfortable in business is often the opening paragraph of its death certificate.*

In my eyes, being comfortable and being complacent are in the same zip code, and that's simply not the right place to live for your business to thrive. Matter of fact, comfort is the last thing an astute entrepreneur should be striving for. More often than not, that feeling moves a business closer to extinction than to a profitable future.

That reality clicked for me the first time I heard Tom Peters remind us that if your business is not broken, you should be willing to break it yourself. Because while you may be enjoying today's success, your competitors are actively searching for tomorrow's advantage.

And they are not trying to copy you. They are committed to replacing you.

So should you not, at the very least, force yourself through that same exercise?

Too many business owners wait for noticeable pain before they acknowledge the need to change. Declining sales. Shrinking margins. New competition. Customer complacency. By the time those signals are impossible to ignore, your options, if any remain, are already severely limited.

Speaking of binge-watching on a cold night, Reed Hastings and Netflix provide one of the clearest modern examples of intentional self-disruption. Self-disruption with a high-profile board and a massive amount of stockholders to keep happy.

Netflix did not wait for DVDs to fail. Embracing the newfangled concept of streaming, they walked away from a profitable DVD-by-mail business while customers were still satisfied and revenue was still strong. That decision was not obvious. It was uncomfortable. It was bold. But it was necessary.

Then Netflix disrupted itself again.

Once streaming proved viable, the company doubled down by investing heavily in original content. That move angered partners, confused investors, and required massive capital. But Hastings understood how to approach Rule #1. Owning the customer relationship was not enough. Netflix needed to own the customer experience.

Every one of these decisions weakened something that was working in order to build something that would last longer.

This type of thinking is likely to feel dangerous. That reaction is understandable. Breaking a business model threatens identity. It challenges ego. It forces leaders to admit that yesterday's wins can quietly become tomorrow's anchors. But keep in mind that when you signed up as an entrepreneur in the first place, that certainty was never on the menu.

I am not talking about recklessness, but rather about being strategic, being innovative, and being willing to take calculated risks.

Businesses rarely fail because leaders are reckless. *They fail because leaders become protective.* Protective of processes. Protective of products. Protective of what they are today.

I am not suggesting you blow everything up. But I am challenging you to question your business model and tactics before the market forces you to. Because when that happens, it is often too late.

At a minimum, create strong hypotheticals and develop intelligent responses. If you could no longer sell online, how would you survive? If your town shut down your drive-through, how would you replace that volume? If you had to cut staff by half, what would you change? If your competitor began opening nights and weekends, how would you respond? If you were no longer legally allowed to sell your highest-grossing product, how would you adapt?

The goal is not reckless reinvention. *It is intentional evolution.* Testing before you have no other choice. Challenging before complacency sets in. Changing by design, not by desperation. And feeling good about yourself and your company in the process.

Waiting until your company is forced to innovate or die is not a strategy. It is simply a slow surrender. That can't possibly be good. Agree?

S2L: The most dangerous version of your business is the one you refuse to question and refuse to reinvigorate. Do not get comfortable. Stay vigilant in your effort to remain ahead of the curve. How else can you protect tomorrow's profitability?

#41 EMBRACE TECHNOLOGY TO PROTECT YOUR COMPANY'S FUTURE.

"Once a new technology rolls over you, if you're not part of the steamroller, you're part of the road." —*Stewart Brand*

There are many reasons I shared a quote from Grace Hopper, one of the first and most legendary computer scientists, before you ever arrived at this book's first chapter. She warned about the danger of continuing to do things the way they have always been done. That warning has never resonated more with astute entrepreneurs than it does today.

Most business owners say they want to grow. Fewer want to change. Even fewer want to learn new technology.

That is ironic. And short-sighted.

Why? *Because technology has quietly become the greatest profit multiplier available to virtually every business on earth, regardless of size, industry, or budget.*

The old excuses many of us cling to no longer apply. "Those guys can afford that stuff, we can't." The tools that once required deep pockets, massive teams, or expert programmers now fit in your pocket. Many cost less than your monthly latte bill. Or at least, mine.

Which tools? The ones that eliminate busywork. The ones that increase accuracy. The ones that free your people to focus on what your customers actually care about.

So why do so many businesses hold on to outdated systems, old processes, and yesterday's ways of working long after they stop adding value?

The truth is simple. Too many owners fear technology. Some have convinced themselves that it will put them out of business. Some believe that their personal inability to take advantage of it will leave them at the mercy of their employees. And others simply can't relate to Grace Hopper's insightful perspective.

For the very small percentage of companies still profiting from outdated inefficiencies, their fear might be justified. But for the overwhelming majority of entrepreneurs, the real target of new technology is not your business.

It is your inefficiency.

So why do so many owners run away from platforms that would make them faster, stronger, and more profitable? Are they worried that technology will expose the weaknesses they have chosen to ignore? Is it concern that today's tools are just too complex to understand?

Fear not. Some of today's tools will literally teach you how to use them. As you're using them.

Technology won't replace your people. It will elevate them. By removing low-value tasks, it will allow your team to spend more time creating experiences, building relationships, and delivering better outcomes for the people who pay your bills.

You should also welcome the fact that technology will empower you to analyze product mix, costs, and profitability with far greater clarity. Many of the metrics this book highlights promise to become dramatically easier to understand and manage with the right tools in place.

If adopting new technology still feels overwhelming, consider this. Your competitors are already adopting it. Your customers already expect it. Your employees are already clamoring for it.

Nothing destroys morale faster than forcing talented people to work inside outdated systems that slow them down, frustrate them, and make every day feel like an uphill battle.

Technology is not an expense. It is a very clear signal. It tells your team that you value their time. Used correctly and with your customers as the priority, it tells them that you value their experience. And it tells the marketplace that your business plans to be in the mix for a long time.

The companies that thrive in the next decade will not be the ones with the biggest budgets or the flashiest tools. They will be the ones that deliver the best and are the most willing to experiment, willing to learn, and willing to evolve. The kind of companies Grace Hopper would have admired.

Your people will stop asking, "Do we have to use this?" and start asking, "Can this take us even further in improving customer satisfaction and employee efficiency?"

If you want to grow, you must embrace the forces that make growth easier. Technology is no longer optional for any company looking to maximize its efficiency. And its bottom line.

S2L: Technology eliminates what holds your people back. Technology lifts your customer, your team, and your bottom line.

#42 BEWARE OF THESE SILENT KILLERS.

"Hope is not a strategy." —*Vince Lombardi*

Too many businesses have two silent killers hiding in plain sight. They don't show up on your profit and loss statements with flashing red lights. They don't scream out for attention like an angry customer or a broken AC compressor. But what they do is quietly distort confidence and create a false and expensive sense of security.

Those two killers are dead inventory and unrealistic pipelines. Often masquerading as positive assets, these cause more financial damage than most leaders usually want to acknowledge.

1. *Dead Inventory: Where profits go to die*

Dead inventory is anything you bought, built, or created that isn't moving. Not selling. Not turning. Not delivering value. Not generating cash.

It just sits there. Taking up space. Tying up your precious capital. Getting older by the day and less valuable by the minute.

Most leaders drastically overestimate the value of their dead inventory. Why? Because they look at what something originally cost instead of what it's currently worth today. They become emotionally attached to the idea that "it'll sell eventually." At retail price, no less. No chance.

So many retailers that I've worked with want to count last year's dresses as full-value inventory. Keep in mind that they couldn't sell them...last year. Yet, at season's end, they still want to overinflate the wholesale value of this year's cases of XS neon orange polo shirts, even though not one of them moved at retail price.

Dead inventory doesn't just cost money. It hides the truth. From you and your CFO or accountant. It gives you the illusion that you have resources of real value when what you really have is sunk cost with a dying pulse or no pulse at all.

Dead inventory slows reaction time. It blocks the products customers actually want. It eats up valuable warehouse space. And it allows you to continue to think you can make chicken salad out of last year's chicken feathers.

Dead inventory is not a storage problem. It's a leadership problem. If it isn't selling, you have only three choices:

1. Discount it.
2. Destroy it.
3. Donate it.

Because keeping it is the costliest decision of all. On SO many levels.

2. Unrealistic Pipelines: The lie we salespeople like to tell ourselves

If dead inventory kills your cash, an unrealistic pipeline can kill your confidence and destroy your cash flow.

Pipelines filled with "maybes," "somedays," and "if the stars align" deals create a dangerous illusion: future revenue that doesn't actually exist and never will come to fruition.

You know the type of pipelines I'm talking about:

• The deal that's been "95 percent sure" for six months
• The prospect who "loves what you do" but never signs
• The customer who says "check back next quarter" every quarter

• The giant proposal sitting on someone's desk in "review" since last St. Patrick's Day

When pipelines become wish lists, decision-making becomes fantasy.

It's easy to get sucked in. A client of mine worked hard to earn the trust of a company with more than three thousand drivers. It was their hope to supply each of those drivers with something of value. As soon as the client showed interest, their reported pipeline immediately included those thousands of potential new users. That made for a heckuva attention-getting pipeline. Well, the client came through...and equipped 100 drivers total on a one-year trial. Uh, oh! Yep, their pipeline was off a whole bunch of zeros. That certainly changed cash flow projections.

An overinflated pipeline is really rat poison. Why? Teams overspend. Leaders overstaff. Owners relax. Budgets inflate. Reality shrinks. And investors scream. Loudly.

An unrealistic pipeline insulates you from the truth that:

Your pricing might be off.

Your follow-up might be weak.

Your offer might not resonate.

Your sales process might be broken.

Your assumptions might be outdated.

Pipelines should never be measured by how full they look. Once you and your sales team are held accountable for what those pipelines actually do and don't produce, everyone automatically becomes more realistic from that day forward.

So why do these two killers often show up together?

Because dead inventory and unrealistic pipelines have the same root cause: avoiding the truth because the truth is uncomfortable. But leaders who refuse to confront reality pay for it in a big way when the consequences arrive. And they will arrive.

The cure is clear: reality, discipline, and action. Evaluate and forecast based on evidence, not emotion. Being optimistic is admirable. But being insulated from the truth is deadly.

S2L: You cannot scale on illusions. You cannot grow on wishful thinking. You cannot build a profitable business on numbers and opportunities that exist only in your head.

#43 DON'T IGNORE THE BORING STUFF.

"Good compliance is good business." —*Preet Bharara*

Almost all the entrepreneurs I work with are obsessed with sales, marketing, and product development. It's only natural for them to worry that any likely downfall they'll ever face will come from a lack of customers or a bad financial decision.

The irony?

For too many, the most damaging and most unprofitable blows will come from the things they assumed they could simply "wing."

Things like payroll. Legal responsibilities. Classification. Hiring. Firing. Building codes. Documentation. Safety precautions. Certification. You get where I'm going, correct?

We all agree it's very possible to recover from a bad revenue month. But a lawsuit, an audit, a temporary shutdown, or an avoidable employee-related mistake can wipe out profits for an entire year. Or worse yet, force you to liquidate.

Every business, regardless of size, faces the same base-level legal and HR responsibilities. You cannot outrun them. You cannot ignore them. You cannot claim to be exempt because you are "too small," "too new," or "too busy."

The IRS doesn't care. The Department of Labor doesn't

care. Your state's tax division doesn't care. Your city's building inspectors don't care. OSHA doesn't care. And plaintiff attorneys definitely don't care.

What they do care about are the gaps in your processes that you probably considered minor. But those very gaps can quietly drain profit, create unnecessary risk, and expose your business to costs you never budgeted for. Or worse yet, shut you down.

The "boring stuff" isn't a distraction from growth. It's part of the profitability formula.

It's actually the stuff that protects the money you work so hard to earn. If you're not sure, seek professional advice and/or assistance. Because nothing is more expensive than screwing up in a big way.

S2L: Profitability isn't just about making more. It's about preventing the costly mistakes that can take it away.

#44 DON'T LET THE IDEA OF SERIAL ENTREPRENEURSHIP DERAIL YOUR SUCCESS.

"Growth for the sake of growth is the ideology of the cancer cell." —*Edward Abbey*

Multiple times throughout this book, I've tried to remind you that *more isn't always better.* In life and in business. After all, would you rather have 3 mediocre homes in three so-so locations or your dream house on the water or in the mountains? Would you rather be served a half dozen store-bought cookies or two of your favorite chocolate chip cookies made with love?

Why then do so many business owners become obsessed with becoming self-proclaimed *"serial entrepreneurs"*? Why do so many successful business owners take their eye off the incredible business they're building to try to duplicate that success again and again with an entirely new-to-them concept? And why the need to label that behavior at all?

I'm never about discouraging anyone from building a business, but all too often the desire to have more and different ventures can unknowingly turn them into "serial business killers." Take one of my most intriguing client relationships with a man who had spent 30 years building an industry-leading business. As he reached his late 50s, he felt the need to build another in a totally unrelated field. Within 24 months, the whiteboard in this office showed the eight other businesses he was in the midst of developing as well as his ideas for two beyond those. I was hired to help with the launch of all of them. It wasn't long before it became obvious to me that his primary business, his "cash cow," was no longer getting anywhere near the attention it had gotten for the past 3 decades.

My advice was for him to slow down on opening up new ventures and refocus on the legacy business he had built. As a result, I was quickly viewed as a cynic. Fast forward 18 months, and I became a visionary. All of his businesses were now unsettled.

That story is not unique. Many of my former Burger King franchisees learned a similar lesson. After exerting themselves to open new concepts, they quickly found themselves trying to recapture the momentum their original franchises had lost.

The obsession with earning the serial entrepreneur label never ceases to amaze me. My advice is not to be "one and done." It is to finish what you start. No entrepreneur should look beyond their first business until it is financially successful, systemized, culturally strong, and supported by the right team. Only then should a second concept be considered.

Too many entrepreneurs are in a race to have the most. Although those misguided dreams help keep me busy as a consultant, I am partial to business people in a race to be the best. That's because great entrepreneurs don't chase volume. They chase excellence.

S2L: Business success requires laser focus. Without it, your team loses motivation, your customers notice lapses in your attention to detail, and your CFO will quickly spot your eroding margins. Every business you own deserves to be treated like it's the only one you possess...because your financial success depends on it.

#45 FINANCE YOUR GROWTH WITH YOUR EYES OPEN.

"Debt is like any other trap, easy enough to get into but hard enough to get out of." —*Josh Billings*

Most entrepreneurs I meet spend a great deal of time searching for capital. For a launch. For inventory. For a warehouse addition. For new equipment. For that dream second location. And that is only the beginning of the financing conversation.

I get it. Entrepreneurs love momentum. They love growth. They love possibility. But too many forget one critical truth. None of it matters if the financing behind it destroys profitability. Growth without profit is not growth. It is a costly illusion.

Yet, often entrepreneurs rush into financing deals that look like jet fuel but behave like boat anchors. Without a trusted advisor or real borrowing experience, they accept money that is too expensive, too restrictive, or too risky because *they believe any funding is better than no funding.*

Flat out...it isn't.

I have benefited from good funding and suffered through terrible funding. It is far easier than you think to take the wrong deal. Yet, bad financing will crush profitability long before it crushes the business. In fact, more companies fail from bad funding than from bad ideas.

Here is the reality. Every dollar you take comes with a cost. The only question is whether that cost leaves you with thicker profits or thinner ones. If a deal looks too easy or too fast or comes with pressure to sign immediately, slow down. Predatory deals rarely announce themselves. The terms tell the story.

I worked with a first-time business owner who was thrilled his bank had approved a startup loan despite his lack of experience and the absence of a business plan. What he did not realize was that the bank had not lent his business anything. They had placed a second mortgage on his aging parents' home and routed the funds to him. His excitement disappeared instantly. So did his peace of mind.

When financing damages your foundation, profitability is no longer part of the discussion. Bad financing destroys profit in many ways:

- Rates that suffocate cash flow
- Covenants that force short-term decisions and long-term damage
- Balloon payments that hit just as stability arrives
- Partners who disrupt operations and dilute focus
- Short-term loans with punishing terms that block profitable growth

Find yourself in one of these situations, and your dream may quickly become your nightmare and someone else's asset. Even worse, revenues may rise while profits collapse. That is the silent tragedy of bad financing. You grow yourself into the red.

Do not overreact to a radio ad. Do not grab the first approval. Do your homework. If the only deal you qualify for is a bad one, ask yourself a hard question. Is it smarter to wait and protect profitability or rush forward and destroy it?

Financing should expand your future. Strengthen your profit engine. Provide time, stability, and breathing room.

Not shrink it. And certainly not sink it.

S2L: Unless you are an experienced financial and legal professional, work with someone who is. Every financing decision either fuels profitability or quietly erases it.

#46 UNDERSTAND THE IMPACT OF YOUR PERSONAL GUARANTEE.

"There is no practice more dangerous than that of borrowing money." *—George Washington*

After decades of owning my own businesses, it is fair to say I have experienced nearly every stage of the entrepreneurial life cycle. Along the way, I have come to realize that the three most impactful words an entrepreneur can hear may be, "Just sign here."

What entrepreneur does not relish momentum? You probably love the rush of building, expanding, upgrading, or launching the next phase of your dream. And nothing fuels momentum faster than borrowed money.

Banks know it. Lenders know it. Factors and vendors benefit from it. That helps to explain why the process is designed to feel painless.

Until you are asked to sign one final document. The personal guarantee.

Everyone advancing you money, and many advancing you products or services before being paid in full, wants to protect their downside. Frankly, you would do the same.

With lenders fully aware that hundreds of thousands of businesses close their doors every year, odds are you will be asked repeatedly during your entrepreneurial journey to provide a personal guarantee.

That personal guarantee exists because lenders are rarely willing to take a risk on your business alone, especially if it lacks a long, solid, and verifiable profit history. They want you all-in personally. Your assets. Your credit. Your livelihood.

That is why signing a personal guarantee is not a business decision. It is a life decision. You are putting yourself on the line. All of you. Your home. Your savings. Your retirement. Your family's financial safety net.

The moment your pen hits the page, all of it becomes collateral.

If the business thrives, great. If the business collapses, you are still legally on the hook.

Most entrepreneurs are convinced their business will not fail, or they never would have launched it. But businesses do not fail on schedule.

They fail during recessions. They fail because of weather events. They fail due to unexpected competition. They fail when equipment breaks down. They fail when a key employee leaves for a competitor. They fail when a major deal falls apart. They fail when a pandemic shows up unannounced.

A personal guarantee means every one of those surprises now follows you home.

That guarantee will likely affect:

- Your future borrowing power
- Your personal credit score
- Your ability to obtain or refinance a mortgage
- Your risk profile with other lenders
- Your business partner or spouse financially tied to you

In rare cases, you may be able to soften a personal guarantee. But that outcome is uncommon.

Take advice from someone who, at age 29, had personally guaranteed what would equal roughly $7M in company debt in today's dollars. Understand exactly what you are agreeing to. Because one thing you will absolutely be adding to your entrepreneurial backpack is pressure. A lot of it.

Most entrepreneurs have no choice but to borrow money in one form or another at some point. At a minimum, honor these non-negotiables.

Know what you are signing. Assess the true risk. Determine whether you can borrow less. And NEVER sign a document like this without a legal professional reviewing it first.

A personal guarantee is another example of why most successful entrepreneurs literally go all in.

S2L: A personal guarantee is not just a business risk. It is a rock-solid personal promise. Treat it with the seriousness your future and your family's future deserve.

#47 BE SMARTER. NOT BUSIER.

"It is not enough to be busy; so are the ants. The question is: What are we busy about? —*Henry David Thoreau*

This book consistently calls for counterintuitive thinking. Few ideas make that need clearer than this one.

Somewhere along the way, being busy became a badge of honor in business. It should not have. You know exactly what that looks like. Long hours. Packed calendars. Endless emails. Back-to-back meetings. Late-night list making. Early-morning texts.

We confuse relentless activity with dedication and commitment. I used to do that, too.

Earlier in the book, I shared a story about being forced to sit and observe my Burger King restaurant during a busy lunch rush with my franchise district manager beside me. Only once, when a fifty-person bus descended on the restaurant, did he allow me to jump up and help address the unexpected demand.

I immediately ran to the kitchen and started feeding more burgers down the broiler. I stayed busy until the rush subsided. I felt great about my effort.

Until he calmly explained the flaw in my approach.

"You got busy and became the tenth person on the shift," he said. "At best, you increased efficiency by about ten percent in that moment. But had you acted as a leader, you could have doubled your team's efficiency and reduced costly food waste."

He explained that if I had first identified the types of orders the group would place and where bottlenecks were likely to occur, I would have seen that many customers were simply ordering drinks. The drink station, not the broiler, was the real constraint. He also pointed out that my approach left us with far too many cooked burgers unsold and destined for the waste bucket.

Running around felt exhilarating. I was busy. I felt useful. And I did not even earn a participation trophy from him.

That lesson has stayed with me.

I still work with business owners who feel constantly overwhelmed and believe that comes with the territory. It does not. And it should not.

Being absurdly busy is usually a signal. And most of what it signals is not admirable. A business stretched too wide. A lack of clear priorities. Broken processes. Inferior training. Poor communication. Ineffective delegation. And yes, poor management.

I routinely see owners solving the same problems again and again instead of identifying and fixing the root cause.

It is easy to confuse activity with progress. Motion feels productive. Constant motion feels hyper-productive. But awareness and efficiency build profit. Motion does not.

Here is a simple guideline. If a task does not improve customer experience, revenue, margin, or scalability, stop making it a priority. It may feel necessary. It may feel urgent. But it is not strategic.

Ask yourself these questions regularly:

If I stopped doing this, would anyone notice? Does this task directly improve customer value, employee efficiency, or profit? Am I doing this because it matters or because it is familiar?

Could someone else do this just as well or better? How could I make more effective use of my time?

If you continue to treat busyness as a virtue, here is what you can expect:

Strategic thinking will always be postponed.

- High-value work will be crowded out by low-value tasks.
- Decisions will remain reactive instead of intentional.
- Mistakes will increase.

And maybe most importantly, burnout, yours and your team's, will accelerate.

If these questions make you uncomfortable, that is a good sign. You are probably onto something important.

Stop measuring success by how full your days are. Start measuring it by how effectively your time and your team's time convert into results that are consistent with your goals.

S2L: Greater profits do not come from doing more. They come from doing better. Replace being busy with working smarter.

SECTION 5

Determine How Customers Best Experience You.

#48 KNOW EXACTLY WHAT YOUR BRAND IS...AND WHAT IT'S NOT.

"A brand is not what you say it is. It's what they say it is."
—*Marty Neumeier*

Most businesspeople believe their brand is their logo, their official colors, their story, their tagline, their packaging, and/or their product features. They would be wrong.

Understanding what a brand truly is requires a return to Rule #1.

Your brand is what your customers believe you are because of how you actually deliver on what you told them to expect. That means you cannot design your way to a brand. You cannot talk your way into a brand.

You earn your brand. Good or bad.

Brands do not build trust. They do not build loyalty. They do not build margin.

Actions do.

That does not at all minimize the importance of your presentation or the features your products or services offer. It simply means your brand is defined by how your customers feel before, during, and after doing business with you. *Not what they think. What they feel.*

Your brand is being built every day by how you handle success and failure. By how you respond to mistakes, refunds, delays, angry customers, stressed employees, and unexpected surprises.

If your customer experience wanes, based on cash flow, staffing shortages, or volume, you still have a brand. Just not the one you want.

Brand is not how well people know you. It is why they choose you. Or why they do not.

Brand is built and protected by establishing your non-negotiables and never straying from them. By staying relentlessly focused on the customer journey. By consistently training and motivating your team. By standing behind every promise you make and every promise you have already made.

Never forget that every interaction either strengthens or weakens your brand. From how the phone is answered. To how intuitive your website feels. To how employees treat one another in front of customers. To how available your company makes itself after a sale.

So ask yourself this question honestly: Are you comfortable with what your brand says about your company?

S2L: Brand must be earned every day. Your job is to deliver the behavior, the experience, and the consistency that lead customers to the conclusion you want. An inferior brand can only produce inferior profits.

#49 PRESENT YOUR BUSINESS WITH PURPOSE.

"The aim of marketing is to know and understand the customer so well the product sells itself." —*Peter Drucker*

You're probably growing tired of hearing me say this, but I'm not ready to back down. *Owning or operating a successful business comes only as a result of maximizing customer satisfaction.*

So why do so many companies miss the mark so badly when it comes to their business name, their product names, their logo, their color palette, their packaging, and *maybe* most importantly, their message?

I know the urge is strong to honor your children or yourself when naming your construction company. I understand why using your favorite NFL team's colors might seem harmless. And who can blame you for letting your sixteen-year-old niece help design your logo? After all, do you really need a marketing professional when there are countless $99 all-in-one solutions showing up in your Facebook feed?

Yes, you do.

Names and logos shape perception. Colors influence emotion and behavior. Messaging affects everything. Website appeal and functionality directly impact sales. And for many businesses, packaging may be just as important as any of the above.

Names matter. Burger King helped launch one of America's most prolific fast-food burger brands more than seventy years ago. But take it from someone who lost a lot of money trying; to this day that moniker has not attracted an ample flood of break-fast customers. (Fortunately, you could make a good living while still losing that day part.)

When a client of mine once wanted to name their software platform using initials that spelled the word DIVA, I had to remind them that that name conveyed an entirely different message than they intended. Fortunately, they listened. And if you plan to name your accounting firm Daniel Island Tax and Accounting, ask yourself whether sounding like a hundred other nearby firms is really a bold move.

Color matters too. The orange and blue of the Denver Broncos do not subliminally encourage anyone to eat. And that abstract logo you bought on Fiverr may not clearly communicate why a customer's life is better with your business in it.

Then there's your website. For many businesses, the goal has simply been to "get one up." Not a site that educates or moti-vates. Not one that performs beautifully across every device. Not one that makes the buying journey intuitive and frictionless. Just one that checks the box.

And messaging likely matters most of all. If your customer is currently not the hero of your story, we've got some serious work to do. Your message must resonate from the very first moment someone becomes aware you exist. They need to immediately understand how you make their life better.

For those of you who use packaging, understand this. America's most successful companies treat packaging as a strategic weapon, not an afterthought. It should be as much a part of your message as any spoken or written word.

I've consistently seen businesses offering mediocre products or services flourish because they were presented exceptionally well. Imagine the results you could achieve if your superior offerings were presented with the same forethought, care, and attention to detail.

Matter of fact, some of the most rewarding work I do is help clients with exceptional products or services present their story in a way that finally matches their value. I find that especially gratifying.

S2L: Customers don't first buy what you sell. They first buy how it's presented. Present poorly, and you are leaving lots of dollars on the table.

#50 LEVERAGE A CUSTOMER BASE THAT ISN'T YOURS...YET.

"If you want to go fast, go alone. If you want to go far, go together." —*African Proverb*

I hate one-offs. There, I said it.

A one-off approach focuses on winning a single customer at a time. That might work if your business is selling nine-million-dollar custom homes. Odds are, you're not.

And that approach certainly would not have worked when I was tasked with launching a AAA professional hockey team in a non-TV market.

We were operating out of a beautiful arena that seated more than 11,000 people. No problem, right? Except we had to try and fill it for 40 home games a season, plus playoffs. And we were starting with roughly 1,000 season ticket holders, a limited marketing budget, and no local television coverage showing highlights or even reporting scores.

Fortunately, my years leading up to pro sports taught me an invaluable lesson. Smart growth often comes from standing on the shoulders of organizations that already have an audience. Had we not done that, our team would have followed all those unsuccessful teams that preceded us. Fact.

Yet most entrepreneurs never think this way.

They assume they must build and grow an audience from scratch. They forget that another business already owns a river of customers flowing right past them. That another organization already serves the exact people they want to reach. That a company definitely exists that employs thousands of people who might benefit from what they sell.

Smart entrepreneurs learn to ride those rivers.

Align with someone who already serves your ideal customer. They invested the time. They spent the money. They earned the trust. Your job is to bring something that makes them look even better to the people they already serve.

That requires knowing the business you're really in and the value you deliver. When you get that right, partnerships feel natural, not forced.

But leverage only works when the customer wins first.

This is not poaching. It is not trickery. It is not backdoor selling. It is value creation. You make life easier, more enjoyable, or more effective for the customer. When you do that, growth accelerates quickly.

You trade slow depth for a faster ascent. Trust me. It's a path worth exploring regularly.

S2L: Welcome growth that comes from standing next to the right people. Lots of companies die seeking one client at a time.

#51 FIND THE BEST WAYS TO TAP INTO THEIR EXISTING AUDIENCE.

"Your network is your net worth." —*Porter Gale*

There are several simple, underutilized ways to leverage other people's audiences. Here are six that work across a wide array of industries.

1. *Strategic partnerships*: Partner with a business that serves the same customer. Co-host, bundle, or collaborate in a way that improves the customer experience. Example: A new veterinarian partners with a local pet food store to welcome new clients.
2. *Referral or ambassador programs:* People love recommending things that make them look helpful or informed. Give them a reason to make it easy. Example: Reward a current customer for a referral and welcome the new one with an incentive.
3. *Cross-promotions:* Two businesses. One customer base. Mutual upside. Example: A gym and a nutrition coach successfully promote each other.
4. *Guest content and borrowed platforms:* Let someone else's credibility introduce you. Example: A sporting goods

store partners with a respected local pickleball expert to launch a new category.

5. *Preferred vendor relationships:* Become the brand another business recommends automatically. Example: An RV dealer partners with a local tire company to better serve customers.

6. *Group sales opportunities:* Organizations constantly look for ways to reward employees or members. Example: Selling game tickets through a large employer's HR department. Better yet, having that company buy a block of tickets for an employee recognition night.

One important caveat: Every partnership must be ethical and mutually beneficial. They will absolutely fail if ego takes over. They thrive when customers feel served and partners feel supported.

Why does this work so well?

Trust is expensive to earn and slow to build. When you partner with a business or organization that people already admire, you inherit that trust immediately. Acquisition costs drop. Reach expands. Growth compounds.

So does profit.

S2L: Customers gained through trusted partners are far more likely to stay, spend, and advocate.

#52 USE LIMITED-TIME OFFERS STRATEGICALLY.

"Opportunities seem more valuable to us when they are less available." —*Robert Cialdini*

I can already hear some of you insisting it is time to widen your slate of offerings. That may be true for some. But I am not convinced the folks at Raising Cane's, with roughly $6.5 million in average unit volume, are eager to add bone-in chicken or pizza to their menu.

Their restraint is intentional.

This is exactly why the strategy of offering LTOs, Limited Time Offers, was born. I learned this firsthand back when I was writing large royalty checks to Burger King every month.

LTOs let customers react without forcing you to commit. They allow the market to speak before you lock anything in. And when done well, they can deliver a temporary boost to both your top and bottom line.

An LTO is not about creativity for creativity's sake. It is a controlled experiment. A low-risk way to test demand, generate urgency, and potentially drive short-term sales, all while protecting focus.

Think McRib.

Think a limited-edition Ford Mustang.

Think a special edition Life is Good t-shirt.

Scarcity creates attention. Attention creates urgency. And urgency often produces a sales bump from both new and returning customers.

But the real value of an LTO is not just the short-term lift. *It is the insight.*

LTOs reveal what customers actually want, which price points resonate, and where operational friction exists. That matters because expanding your permanent offering is expensive. It increases training. It complicates inventory. It creates waste risk.

Too many businesses skip testing and expand product offerings immediately, only to learn that their enthusiasm did not translate into sustainable customer demand.

When an LTO works, you now have evidence to justify adding that item or service long-term.

When it works just well enough, you can bring it back later, benefiting again from renewed interest and incremental sales.

And when it fails to meet your goals, the clock simply runs out. You move on. No explanation required. Had that same item been added permanently and flopped, the damage created would have been far greater.

Used correctly, LTOs add interest without diluting identity. Many of your regular customers will rush in to try something new. But discipline matters. If customers cannot quickly connect the offer to why they already trust you, you have gone too far.

And if you feel the urge to expand your ongoing offerings, test first. Let customers vote with their wallets. Then decide.

S2L: Smart businesses understand the power of LTOs. They provide invaluable customer feedback and can deliver an immediate bump in both sales and profit without sacrificing focus.

#53 DON'T RELY ON DISCOUNTING.

"Don't think of cost. Think of value." —*John Spence*

Another counterintuitive thought to ponder: How can discounting possibly be bad if it drives sales?

Discounting feels normal. Generous. Even effective. But much of the time, it is simply the fastest...and unfortunately the most effective...way to erode margin, weaken positioning, and train customers to wait for future price concessions.

There is a smarter alternative, one that is employed far too infrequently.

Instead of lowering your price, add a tangible benefit with real retail value. Something the customer clearly understands and appreciates, while your actual price remains in place. The customer experiences more value. And you preserve your pricing integrity. Everyone wins.

This is nuanced marketing at its finest.

It is not about throwing in something random. It is about offering an add-on that reinforces why the customer chose you in the first place. Something useful. Something relevant. Something you can confidently assign a stated value to. Something that may even create a trial of a product or service the customer might never have experienced otherwise.

A friend of mine is a buyer for Skechers. She raves about the buying experience but rarely mentions price. When I asked why, her answer was immediate.

"When I get that bag with my new shoes and realize it's also a backpack, I think that's brilliant. It feels like a bonus."

That's the point. Value is remembered long after discounts are forgotten. And the math favors you.

Discounts reduce revenue dollar for dollar. Value-adds reduce revenue only by their cost. That distinction matters. A lot.

A fifteen percent discount permanently shrinks the economics of the entire sale. A value-add preserves the full price while creating the emotional feeling of getting more than expected. Customers don't feel like they "won" because you caved. They feel rewarded because you cared.

It gets worse.

When discounting becomes regular...or worse, predictable... customers quickly learn how to never again pay full price. That spells trouble. In a big way.

I once watched a fellow team president discount the heck out of weeknight tickets in hopes of getting more people to experience game action on those perpetually slow nights in minor league sports. It seemed natural enough. But the results were absolutely disastrous. The discounts barely increased attendance, in part because poor midweek turnout had very little to do with price. In reality, all he accomplished was collecting less money from people who were already planning to attend. Worse still, the discounts forced him to provide substantial rebates to existing season-ticket holders. He would have been much better offering a better weeknight game experience to all in hopes of nudging on-the-fence attendees to attend on an off-night.

Need more evidence of the perils of consistent discounting?

A local bowling proprietor wanted more weeknight activity.

In search of a quick fix, he essentially gave away Tuesday night bowling. And it worked. Or so it seemed.

What actually happened? Much of their full-price Monday, Wednesday, and Thursday business simply migrated to discounted Tuesday night. Worse still, the price gap between Tuesday night bowling and Saturday night bowling became so large that weekend bowlers felt they were being overcharged.

So what kind of value-add offer could have achieved the original goal without damaging the business?

How about a free $5 snack bar credit for every $15 spent on Tuesday night bowling? Or a buy two games on Tuesday and get a free game on Thursday offer? The customer feels rewarded, you get paid in full, and the cost of the incentive is minimal.

That is penny-profit thinking in action.

When you add value instead of cutting price, you protect margin, reinforce positioning, and avoid cheapening your brand. You also maintain optionality. Value-adds can be repeated, refined, or rotated. Discounts, once introduced, are hard to take back.

If a customer pushes back on price, resist the urge to immediately reach for the eraser. Reach for creativity instead. Ask yourself what additional benefit would matter to them, carry real perceived value, and cost you far less than the dollars you are being asked to give up.

You may be surprised by what you arrive at.

S2L: Discounts reduce value. Predictable discounting crushes it. Well-conceived value-adds enhance value instead. Protect your price and your bottom line by adding something tangible, not erasing dollars.

#54 TAKE THEIR MONEY THE WAY THEY PREFER.

"We see our customers as invited guests to a party and we are the hosts." —*Jeff Bezos*

Here we go again. Another strong reminder to revisit Rule #1.

As a dear colleague once told me, "Nothing good happens between the time a client says yes and the time you get paid."

If you want more sales, start by eliminating every obstacle that stands between your customer and a completed transaction. One of the most overlooked obstacles in business still today is how customers prefer to pay. Not how you want to be paid. Not how you used to accept payment. How they want to pay at that exact moment.

It sounds painfully simple. Yet far too many businesses unknowingly lose sales because their preferred method of getting paid is completely different from their customer's preferred method of paying.

People abandoned cash years ago. Most abandoned checks. Customers now shift constantly between credit cards, tap-to-pay, digital wallets, Venmo, and similar platforms. Some want in-house financing. Many business customers prefer wire transfers or ACH.

That is because today's customer does not merely desire convenience. They demand it.

They expect speed. They expect options. They expect emailed receipts. And they like reward points and cash-back refunds.

When you make it difficult for people to give you their money, they hesitate. When they hesitate, your chances of closing the sale drop. Sometimes they disappear entirely.

Fast-food operators fought this battle long before most other businesses. For years, franchisees resisted accepting credit cards. They were convinced a 3.5 percent fee would sink them. Had they known that card users were happier, spent twenty to forty percent more than cash customers, and visited more often, they would have embraced cards immediately. I know I would have.

Here is what too many businesses still ignore. Customers hate friction, especially when it comes from the seller. The more friction you add at the moment of payment, the more customers you lose. That is not debatable.

Do not miss the forest for the fees.

If the powerful analogy Jeff Bezos used resonates with you, why would you make it difficult for invited guests to participate in the party you asked them to attend?

Accepting the payment methods your customers prefer is not a technology decision. It is a customer decision. A profitability decision. A growth decision.

It all comes down to this. Are you reducing friction at the exact moment your customer is ready to pay? If not, change it by next Monday. And if you are creating one final hurdle that pushes them toward a competitor, do not wait until Monday.

And if you're still accepting cash only as a strategy to circumvent Uncle Sam, you are destined to lose on multiple fronts.

S2L: When you take their money the way they prefer, you get more of it. When paying you is simple, fast, and

familiar, more happens naturally. Customers buy more, buy more often, and enjoy doing business with you more.

#55 EXPLOIT YOUR ABILITY TO BE NIMBLE.

"When you're small, you can do things that don't scale. That's exactly why they work." —*Paul Graham*

One of the design professionals I work with said something years ago that has stuck with me ever since. When I asked him if he'd ever thought about how he'd like to die, he answered without hesitation.

"By corporate committee," he said. "Yep! It'd take months and months, maybe years, before anything actually happened."

You see, one of the greatest advantages you have as an entrepreneur is also one of the easiest to overlook.

You can move. You can act. You can respond immediately. You can initiate.

Big companies can't.

They study. They form committees. They circulate memos. They protect precedent. By the time they decide what to do, the moment has often passed.

You, on the other hand, can pivot by lunchtime.

So why do so many small companies fail to take advantage of this? Why do they put policies ahead of customers? Why do so few empower employees to do what's right in the moment?

Nimbleness should come from proximity. You are closer to your customer than the big players. Closer to the problem. Closer to the solution. You hear things in real time. You see patterns forming long before they show up in a quarterly report. That's not a weakness. That's your leverage. Or at least it should be.

Large organizations must apply policies evenly. You don't need to.

As a retailer, you can deliver to a regular customer who's sick and can't leave the house, even if delivery isn't normally offered.

As a small contractor, you can extend payment terms to a longtime customer without waiting to run a formal credit report.

As a manufacturer, you can adjust an order, a process, or a promise because the situation calls for it.

As a wedding photographer, you can spend an extra hour taking photos at the bride's infirm grandmother's house without adding a special travel fee.

That's not inconsistency. That's judgment. And it's smart business.

Big companies fear exceptions because exceptions don't scale well. Small companies should embrace them because relationships scale profitably.

You can also create things that simply aren't possible inside a corporate box. A personal menu. A custom offering. A one-off solution that becomes a quiet legend among your best customers.

As I shared earlier, Burger King couldn't allow my restaurant to continue offering blueberry pancakes because they did too well. The moment they succeeded, every nearby location, every franchisee, and every customer expected them everywhere, all the time. Their sheer size as an international behemoth turned creativity into liability.

As an entrepreneur, your size can turn creativity into advantage. You can say yes without breaking the system because you *are* the system.

S2L: Build a company that recognizes nimbleness as a profit strategy. And rewards its implementation.

#56 BEND WHEN YOU SHOULD.

"People will never forget how you made them feel." —
Maya Angelou

Personalize instead of standardize.

Your ability to pivot, personalize, and respond is a competitive advantage that large companies cannot easily copy.

A good friend of mine is about to drive past several dealerships to buy her third Subaru from the same salesperson. His name is Joe. The reason is simple. At one point, he handed her a feather.

She had mentioned, in passing, that she enjoyed collecting feathers. Joe remembered.

Here is how she put it.

"Joe made me feel less like a customer and more like a person. He paid attention. That mattered to me. I will always buy my next car from Joe."

There may be no better example of nimbleness and a customer-first mentality than the now-famous street hot dog story.

Eleven Madison Park in New York City is one of the most celebrated fine-dining restaurants in the world. White tablecloths. Tasting menus. Multiple Michelin stars. Not exactly Hot Dog Central.

One evening, an out-of-town couple was dining when the husband casually mentioned to his server that he regretted not having time to grab his first New York street hot dog before they left town the next morning. No complaint. No expectation. Just a random comment.

The server shared it with the team. Instead of dismissing it, they acted. While the couple continued their multi-course tasting menu, someone quietly left the building, found a street vendor, bought a hot dog, and brought it back to the kitchen.

Minutes later, the server returned with a New York street hot dog, served elegantly on fine china.

No charge. No announcement. No explanation. Just utter disbelief and appreciation.

That's not just good service. That's smart business.

Had my team done that at Burger King, I would have put my franchise at risk. That's the everyone-is-treated-the-same-every-time nature of large organizations on full display.

Here's the real message, loud and clear. Don't drift into the same weaknesses that trap big companies. Don't hide behind rigid rules borrowed from organizations ten times your size. Don't build ultra-rigid processes just to look "professional."

S2L: Every customer, individual or corporate, responds to personalized attention. Your company mantra should make that a priority. Your bottom line will reflect that.

#57 PAY WAY MORE ATTENTION TO RETENTION.

"Retention is the ultimate measure of value delivered."
—Frederick Reichheld

If I could hand you a customer who is likely to spend fifty to seventy percent more than the next customer you acquire, would you want them?

If I could introduce you to an employee whose immediate value is light-years ahead of the next one you'd hire, would you want them, too?

If your answer is a resounding yes, the good news is this. You already have them.

A satisfied, existing customer is gold. So is a trained, motivated employee.

So why do both receive only a fraction of the attention you devote to finding new ones?

Most businesses obsess over acquisition. New customers. New hires. New leads. Growth feels exciting. It's human nature. Retention, by comparison, feels boring. And boring rarely gets the attention it deserves.

Why does retention feel boring? Because it requires daily discipline. Discipline that shows up in small moments such as:

- How quickly problems are addressed
- How often flexibility is offered
- How consistently appreciation is expressed
- How often leaders listen instead of explain

Retention translates to built-in moments that may seem small but compound over time.

Acquisition feels like action. And we Americans love action.

But if success is what you crave, some truths are undeniable. Retention delivers stability. Retention drives profitability. Retention creates longevity.

If you want more loyal customers, pay attention to them. Reward them. Respect them. Overdeliver for them. And just as important, do everything needed to keep the people who serve them.

If you genuinely do want to keep great employees, give them training, recognition, and customers worth serving.

The facts are undeniable. Satisfied customers spend more, return more often, and refer others more regularly. And it costs five times more to replace them than to keep them.

Employee turnover is just as costly. According to Gallup, up to forty-two percent of voluntary turnover is preventable through better management and recognition. Once you factor in the time it takes for a new employee to reach full productivity, the damage to consistent service becomes obvious. No. Better yet, glaring.

If retention sounds boring, fine.

Boring never sounded so profitable to me.

S2L: If actively retaining both customers and employees is not a daily priority for you and your management team, stop pretending you're serious about maximizing profitability.

#58 STRIVE TO BE A GOOD WORLD CITIZEN.

"The price of greatness is responsibility." —*Winston Churchill*

My goal in writing this book has always been to help you become a great entrepreneur. And Churchill makes one thing clear: greatness is never free. It always comes with responsibility.

No entrepreneur operates in a vacuum. Every business lives inside a community, an economy, and a shared world. Whether you acknowledge it or not, your company leaves an imprint.

Does your imprint strengthen what surrounds you... or slowly erode it?

Being a good world citizen is not a marketing exercise. It has nothing to do with slogans, certifications, or social media posts. It's not about looking responsible. It's about being responsible.

Responsible for:

- the people you employ
- the customers who trust you
- the communities that make it possible for you to operate and grow

And here's the part most leaders miss: Responsibility rarely shows up in grand gestures. It shows up in ordinary moments.

In how you treat people who have little leverage.

In whether you exploit customers who don't know better.

In how you respond when something goes wrong.

And most importantly...

In whether you choose restraint when something is legal, profitable... and still wrong.

Too many entrepreneurs dismiss this as idealistic. That's a convenient excuse. This isn't about idealism. It's about character.

And character is revealed when you're staring at a highly questionable alternative that's easier, faster, and more lucrative.

Over the course of my career, I've done my best not to professionally engage with leaders who choose to operate the wrong way. And on the occasions when I allowed myself into even the "gray area," it never ended well. Not once.

Here's the unavoidable truth: as a business leader, every decision you make shapes culture, trust, and expectations. Ignore that reality and the damage doesn't disappear.

It just shows up later—quietly and corrosively: Disengaged employees. Cynical customers. Fractured relationships. Communities that tolerate you, but never support you. And maybe most costly of all...

A personal mindset that never reaches full contentment.

On the other hand, entrepreneurs who act with conscience earn something far more durable than applause.

They earn respect. Employees stay because they're proud of where they work. Customers advocate because they trust how you operate. Partners collaborate because they believe in your intent.

Those outcomes don't just happen. They're earned.

Being a good world citizen doesn't require perfection. It requires awareness, humility, consistency, and accountability. When mistakes happen, and they will, responsible leaders acknowledge them, fix them, and move forward.

Credibility is built through behavior. Not carefully scripted messaging.

As this book winds down, I'm not asking you to choose between doing right and doing well. I'm asking you to recognize something far more important: Doing right is your obligation as a business leader and as a world citizen.

The fact that trust, loyalty, and long-term success often follow isn't the reason to act responsibly. It's the result.

S2L: Do the right thing because it's right. Businesses that act with conscience earn trust, respect, support, and an inner peace they could never buy. Longevity tends to follow. And your personal bottom line will always be stronger for it.

#59 ENJOY SOME FINAL THOUGHTS.

"When you focus on building positive relationships with your customers and your team, performance substantially improves, personal satisfaction grows, and greater profits follow. What's better than that as an entrepreneur?" —*Peter Ricciardi*

Thank you for spending time with me on this journey toward greater profitability and personal satisfaction. I know how valuable your time is, and I don't take that lightly. I'm genuinely honored you chose to spend some of it here.

My hope is simple: that this book helps you think differently... so your desired results can follow. With that in mind, here are a few final thoughts worth carrying with you.

1. *Don't give up.*

Before building Disney, Walt Disney ran an animation company that went bankrupt. He was fired from a newspaper for "lacking imagination." Oprah was told she wasn't fit for television in advance of becoming a media icon. Steve Jobs was fired from Apple, the company he co-founded, before returning to lead it to historic success. Reid Hoffman helped launch

SocialNet before LinkedIn. It failed. Even LinkedIn struggled early. Today, it has over a billion members.

The point isn't the names. The point is the pattern.

2. *You are not alone. Not even close.*

America runs on small business. As of 2025, there are more than 36 million small businesses in the United States. Nearly 44% of U.S. GDP is attributed to them. Roughly 430,000 new business applications are accepted each month.

You are part of something massive. And you have every opportunity to be among the best.

3. *Confidence builds businesses. Ego destroys them.*

Ego convinces entrepreneurs they already have the answers. It rejects data, fuels stubbornness, and blocks adaptability. Worse still, ego poisons culture.

Confidence stays curious. Ego stays certain.

4. *Don't ignore your health.*

Physical well-being affects cognitive performance. When energy drops and stress spikes, decision quality suffers. That's simply a fact.

Your body and your mind are the engines that carry you through this work. Treat them like it. Anything less pulls you farther from your goals, and from the positivity you need to lead well.

5. *Get comfortable with what you don't know. Yet.*

Feel good realizing you're an expert at many things, just not everything. Challenge yourself and your team to keep learning. Seek help in as many forms as possible. And never confuse curiosity with weakness. Curiosity is strength. It's how the best leaders keep getting even better.

It's time to say good-bye. At least, for now.

This book wasn't written to chase a zillion sales. It was written to help you shift your mindset and lift your profits. And to achieve greater personal and professional satisfaction along the way.

I'd truly welcome your feedback. And I'm always open to working with businesspeople like you, leaders who expect more from themselves, refuse to stand still, and believe the best outcomes are the ones where everybody wins.

Until we reconnect, Peter

FINAL OBSERVATIONS AND TAKEAWAYS

BY THE NUMBERS

Entrepreneurship in Context

As an entrepreneur, you are not alone. Nor are the employees who depend on you.

- 45.9% of American workers are employed by small businesses.
- 43.5% of U.S. GDP is generated by small businesses.
- 36.2 million small businesses operate in the United States.
- 430,000 new business applications are filed each month.
- 14.2 million U.S. businesses are women-owned, producing $2.8 trillion in receipts.
- 9% of small employer firms are veteran-owned.
- 2 in 3 entrepreneurs self-fund their businesses.

Sources available upon request.

THE DIZZYING DOZEN

12 Business Myths That Can Confuse Any Entrepreneur

1. **"If you build it, they will come."**
The real truth: This isn't the movies. Customers don't magically appear. Effective marketing, consistent visibility, and ongoing outreach are almost always required to drive traffic.

2. **"Great products sell themselves."**
The real truth: Plenty of companies with excellent products still fail. Even the best offerings require selling, storytelling, and smart distribution.

3. **"More sales will fix everything."**
The real truth: More sales can actually make things worse when margins are thin, costs are uncontrolled, or additional inventory, labor, or delivery expenses must be incurred long before a dollar is collected.

4. **"Hiring more people makes growth easier."**
The real truth: Quality beats quantity. Growth requires the *right* people, not simply more of them. Payroll added too early can crush cash flow, and undertrained employees can do more damage than being short-staffed.

5. **"Low price always wins."**
The real truth: Price matters far less than perceived

value. Customers buy what feels worth it, not what is cheapest.

6 **"Bigger is always better."**

The real truth: Bigger is only better when it remains focused and efficient. Small and nimble often outperform large and bloated. Scale can dilute speed, efficiency, and customer focus.

7. **"If I just get the systems right, the business will run itself."**

The real truth: Systems matter, but systems without committed people, consistent execution, and ongoing refinement rarely stay "right" for long.

8. **"A wider product line increases my chances of success."**

The real truth: Too much choice creates confusion, waste, and inefficiency. You win when customers clearly understand what you do best.

9. **"Being super busy means I'm maximizing productivity."**

The real truth: Busy and efficient are not synonyms. Busyness often signals underpricing, understaffing, disorganization, overcomplication, or poor management.

10. **"Marketing is an expense not all companies can afford."**

The real truth: If people don't know you exist, growth is wishful thinking. Marketing takes many forms and price points, but some form of investment is non-negotiable.

11. **"Success happens quickly when the idea is good enough."**

The real truth: Most "overnight successes" take years. Amazon launched in 1994, posted its first profitable quarter in 2001, and its first profitable year in 2003. Uber took even longer. Consistency and staying power often beat brilliance. There is no fixed timeline to profitability, which is why patience and adequate working capital matter.

12. **"AI will level the playing field for all entrepreneurs."**

The real truth: Few things are more misunderstood than AI and large language models. The more you know about a subject, the more valuable AI becomes. A seasoned home builder will get far better output than a novice because the expert knows what to ask, what to ignore, and how to apply the results.

ENTREPRENEURIAL REALITY CHECKS

- Never convince yourself that anything is more important than your customer's experience.
- Once you lose sight of the details, you are officially in the weeds.
- Angry customers tell their story louder than satisfied ones.
- If your only competitive advantage is price or speed, expect someone to steal it.
- Every business decision must account for customer satisfaction and employee execution.
- Unhappy employees translate directly into unhappy customers.
- It is almost always less expensive to keep a customer than to replace one.
- Never fool yourself about the value of dead inventory or an inflated pipeline.
- Never lose sight of your cash flow or the length of your runway.
- You are not truly your own boss. Customers and employees decide your fate.
- Build your website for your customer, not your ego.
- Customers do not buy features. They buy what benefits them.
- What worked yesterday mattered then. It may be irrelevant tomorrow.

• The cheapest option often proves the most expensive.
• If you do not love what you do, you are far more likely to fail.

PETE-ISMS

1. Your business is what it says it is...until it underdelivers.
2. A niche and a hole often look exactly the same, so do your homework before filling it with cash.
3. Too many people don't want to be confused by the facts.
4. Entrepreneurs are free...to have their eye on their business virtually every minute.
5. Would you work for you?
6. Everyone has the right to be wrong.
7. You can't save your way to success.
8. Going fast doesn't always get you there faster.
9. Winners know what they don't know.
10. Free might not even be convincing enough at that time.
11. Be happy only when you're less important than your customer and your employees.
12. Better should always come before bigger.
13. You can't deposit percentages in the bank.
14. If you think you've got this on your own, reconsider.
15. You've got to play the cards, not the money.

16. It's not what you pay. It's what you get.
17. Too many important business decisions are made by accident.
18. Your elevator speech should not require that you start on the 100th floor.
19. Learn to enjoy learning from your mistakes.
20. Would your mom be proud of the way you approach business?

BGPP: BUSINESS GLOSSARY PER PETE

Definitions without context have little value. Used correctly, they sharpen thinking, improve decision-making, and expose blind spots. This glossary reflects how businesses actually operate, not how spreadsheets or theorists assume they do.

COST, PRICING & PROFITABILITY

Opportunity Cost

The value of the next best alternative you give up when making a decision. It may involve money, time, or focus. (High-performing entrepreneurs consistently weigh tradeoffs.)

Ideal Cost

The theoretical cost of a product or service under perfect conditions with no waste, errors, or inefficiencies. (Extremely useful as a benchmark, it is extremely dangerous when treated as reality.)

Real Cost

The actual cost once waste, spoilage, rework, overtime, theft, and inefficiencies are included. Real cost is always higher than ideal cost. (Ignoring this gap quietly erodes profit while hindering decision-making.)

Pro Forma

A projected financial statement based on assumptions, commonly used for startups, expansions, and investment analysis. (Too often, it is built on ideal instead of real costs.)

Inventory Shrinkage

Loss of inventory due to theft, damage, spoilage, miscounts, or administrative error. (Shrinkage directly reduces profitability.)

Dead Inventory

Inventory that no longer sells or sells extremely slowly. It often requires discounting or disposal to recover value and free working capital. (When hidden or misrepresented, it creates a false sense of strength.)

Percentage Profit

Profit expressed as a percentage of the selling price. Example: $20 profit on a $100 sale equals 20%. (This metric is frequently overemphasized in pricing and incentive programs.)

Penny Profit

Profit expressed as dollars earned per unit sold. Example: "We earn $1.75 per sandwich." (Often ignored, despite its direct impact on cash flow.)

Price Value

The customer's perception of whether the price matches the value received. (Low price value is an early warning sign.)

Product Mix

The combination of products or services a business offers and the sales related to it. Consistent focus on it improves margins, sales, and satisfaction. (It also reveals how customers are behaving.)

Value Add

Any enhancement that increases usefulness or customer benefit beyond basic function. (Adding value usually beats discounting price.)

COST STRUCTURE & LABOR

Fixed Costs

Expenses that do not change with sales volume, such as rent, insurance, and salaried labor. (Identifying these is critical to understanding breakeven.)

Variable Costs

Expenses that fluctuate with sales volume, such as materials, packaging, hourly wages, plus fringe and shipping. (Although not all are controllable, all must be known.)

Variable Margin

Selling price minus variable costs. (The fixed cost vs. variable margin analysis is a cornerstone in calculating breakeven.)

Labor Fringe

Costs beyond wages, including payroll taxes, benefits, vacation, workers' compensation, and retirement. (In the private sector, it is often nearly 30% of wages.)

CASH, CAPITAL & FINANCIAL STABILITY

Cash Flow

Money moving into and out of the business. Positive cash flow allows obligations to be met and growth to be funded. (Unfortunately, strong sales alone do not guarantee strong cash flow.)

Working Capital

Current assets minus current liabilities. (Insufficient working capital can cripple even profitable companies.)

Undercapitalization

Lacking sufficient capital to operate effectively. (This occurrence, common at launch especially, can be fatal.)

Burn Rate

The rate at which cash is consumed, typically measured monthly. (High burn shortens decision time.)

Runway (or Breakeven Runway)

How long a business can operate before cash is exhausted, based on burn rate. (A short runway requires immediate action.)

Overexpansion

Growth that outpaces financial, operational, or managerial capacity. (This is a factor that frequently results in cash and quality problems.)

FRANCHISING

Franchisee

An operator licensed to use a franchisor's brand and systems. (Be reminded that consistency comes at the cost of flexibility.)

Franchisor

The brand owner who licenses the business model in exchange for fees and royalties. (Their revenue and bottom line are driven by their franchisees' top-line sales.)

BRANDING, POSITIONING & STRATEGY

Branding

The intentional creation of a company's identity and promise. (A brand is a perception, not a logo.)

Positioning

The place a business occupies in the customer's mind relative to competitors. (Clarity and consistency are essential.)

Pivot

A deliberate change in strategy, product, pricing, or execution based on new information or market feedback. (Effective pivots are common and intentional, not emotional.)

Competitive Advantage

Strengths that allow a business to outperform competitors. (This status is rarely sustained by low price alone.)

USP (Unique Selling Proposition)

A clear explanation of why customers should choose one business over another. (Operating with the lack of a USP is a major risk.)

Menu Proliferation

Offering too many products or services, increasing cost and complexity. ("Narrower often gets you wider.")

Investment Spending

Capital deployed for future return rather than immediate payoff. (Too often overlooked, these critical expenditures must be mindfully evaluated in advance.)

CUSTOMER METRICS & REVENUE DRIVERS

Metrics

Quantifiable measurements used to evaluate business performance, including sales, profitability, efficiency, and customer behavior. (You cannot manage what you do not consistently measure.)

Customer Acquisition Cost (CAC)

Total cost to acquire a new customer. (When CAC exceeds a customer's lifetime value, growth can actually be destructive.)

Pipeline

A staged view of future sales opportunities or projects moving toward completion. (Overestimating quality or close probability can be extremely costly.)

Customer Count

Total customers or transactions in a defined period. (Sales growth without customer growth is deceptive.)

Trends

Patterns in sales performance over time, including growth, decline, or seasonality. (Accurate trends improve short- and long-term cash flow predictability.)

Average Ticket

Average spend per transaction. (Increases matter only when they reflect greater purchase and simply price inflation.)

Frequency

How often customers purchase over time. (Small gains compound rapidly. Small declines also do so.)

Retention Rate

The percentage of customers who continue doing business over time. (One of the most revealing metrics.)

Churn Rate

The percentage of customers lost in a given period. (High churn demands immediate attention and a thorough explanation.)

Upsell

Encouraging a higher-value purchase. (Boosts penny profit when done correctly.)

Cross-Sell

Encouraging complementary purchases. (This effective tactic is often a win for both business and customer.)

PROFIT & PERFORMANCE

Bottom Line

Net profit after all expenses are deducted from revenue. (This is the goal, unless cash flow problems are quietly undermining it.)

ACKNOWLEDGMENTS

It should be obvious after reading this book that none of us gets through life without the help and support of others. It should also be clear that you cannot take on an undertaking of this magnitude without learning from many people along the way and without being given the privilege of helping others succeed in return.

I have been fortunate that so many people took a leap of faith and gave me opportunities that shaped my path. They include:

• The administration at Pascack Valley High School
No one is offered a teaching and coaching job at age nineteen with college classes still remaining unless people truly believe in you.

• The former leadership of Burger King New England
Who awards a nearly impossible-to-secure franchise to a twenty-five-year-old teacher and coach with zero business experience? They did.

• David Crowley, partner at Wachusett Mountain Ski Area
A wonderfully disruptive thinker, David believed in my value as a profitability and marketing specialist before I fully did myself. He gave me my first true consulting opportunity.

• Roy Boe, founder of the New York Islanders and the New York Nets

Roy handed the keys of an American Hockey League franchise to a basketball and baseball guy because he saw passion, commitment, acumen, and the ability to successfully launch a new professional team in Worcester.

• **Phil Evans, former President of the NBA D-League**
Phil believed I could bring a new perspective to both a team and a fledgling league.

• **Charlie Noonan, longtime friend, fellow coach, and entrepreneur**
Charlie continues to share his wisdom, experience, encouragement, and refusal to accept mediocrity.

• **Jim Van Law, banker, startup builder, and friend**
Jim believed I was the right person to help him build a successful consulting practice in Charleston, where we both still live and continue to work together.

• **Wade and Brett, co-owners of Saltwater Cowboys**
It took real trust for two seasoned food and beverage veterans to seek my help while building what is now one of Charleston's most respected and successful waterfront establishments.

• **Todd Benfield, lead business partner at Coastal RV Center**
Todd welcomed a very satisfied customer into his marketing and positioning world, which led to a friendship and working relationship I deeply value.

• **Don Kassing, Amazon expert and technology consultant**
Whether collaborating on clients or debating strategy and technology, I am always better for the exchange.

• **Lee Zavakos, entrepreneur and business partner**
Lee, my business rock and close friend of nearly fifteen years, has consistently and selflessly shared ideas, insights, and opportunities.

This list could easily continue. Mark O, Gordon, Anir, Lou,

Al, Ashley and Sean, Julie, Jeff, Pete, Mark E, John, Steve, Rich K, Rob, Shawn, Michael, David, Dawn and Mark, Chad and Doc, along with many others, also deserve recognition and my sincere thanks.

www.ingramcontent.com/pod-product-compliance
Lightning Source LLC
Chambersburg PA
CBHW021041130626
46552CB00005B/1959